Chosen to Believe

Angela Grubbs

For my dear friend Natalie –
thank you for all of your
support during my crazy ordeal!
you are a true friend
with much love,

Ang
AKA "FRANCINE"
LOL

PINK ELEPHANT PRESS

JONESBORO, GEORGIA

First Printing, 2006

ISBN 0-9772975-0-0

Library of Congress Control Number: 2005908237

Edited by: L. Michelle Tullier Ph.D.
Interior design by: Agnew's, Inc.
Cover design by: Brion Sausser

PART I

Let's Go Crazy

Old Time Religion

The large harvest moon crests over the small white tent erected by the Forest Baptist Church. It hovers over the eager church members and their tent, whispering promises of a greater future to all who enter. Rows of wooden and metal chairs spread from a center aisle leading to a stage hastily erected with plywood and covered with artificial green turf. The year is 1979.

Church members and those lucky enough to be invited as guests that night have packed the tent, the men in their best plaid suits and women dressed conservatively in long denim skirts with striped blouses. They mingle underneath the tarp eagerly awaiting the sermon. The first two rows of chairs on both sides of the stage are reserved for the children who already know if they do not behave during the sermon, a deacon standing alongside the walls of the tent will lead them out. The deacons have learned the children are easier for the church to control if they are clustered together away from their parents. Little Angela Grubbs, eight years old with thin blonde hair in pig tails, waits anxiously for the sermon to begin.

Angela's entire world fits under this tent, which sits rather awkwardly in the newly paved parking lot next to the empty plain chapel with a large white metal cross on the steeple. Nothing seems to change in her safe, suburban world located just thirty minutes south of the bustling big city of Atlanta, Georgia. Angela attends church here with her family and the church's Christian school with her cousins. She has eight other cousins in the school, four of whom are close to her in age, all of whom make up the row in which she is now seated under the big white tent.

Angela, an only child, enjoys church and thinks of it as a great opportunity to get together with her friends and cousins to play. Lucky for her, the church and school pack their members' schedules with mother-daughter banquets, father-son devotionals, fall festivals, car washes, basketball games, football games and volleyball for the girls. When there isn't a social event, the doors to the church are open for worship.

There's soul-winning for all age groups on Saturdays, Sunday morning and evening church services, Wednesday night service and early morning Sunday school. The children who attend the school have the extra benefit of mandatory chapel every day of the week and a bible class. Two hours a day dedicated to studying and serving the Lord. The parents are truly ecstatic.

Every Sunday after church, Angela and her entire family patronize a local restaurant that serves good old country cooking. They dine on fried chicken, collard greens, and black eyed peas, drink sweet iced tea, and greet other church member families that also stop by. Life tastes really good to little Angela Grubbs. With her family and friends, she learns new bible stories and shares a special bond growing up together in this isolated, safe, Christian-based world.

Looking back at the people entering the tent laughing and speaking to one another, Angela smiles and thinks about the love and happiness surrounding her tonight. She loves the way the preacher and members of the church genuinely care for one another, always asking questions about her family and offering counseling if any situation requires outside assistance. Angela knows if she has a problem, even with her own parents, she need only ask for guidance and the church will be there for her. They promise the children these things during Sunday school and at school during the day. The teachers are just as concerned as the church members.

They care so much for each other that they notice when other members aren't there. Angela saw a list of 'missing' members on a sheet once in the church's office. She discovered that members of the church actually volunteer to call or visit people who have stopped regularly attending church to make sure everything is alright. Angela thinks this is a wonderful idea, and looks forward to the day when she's old enough to volunteer so that people will know she really cares and misses them too.

Angela knows that the church members have rented this tent, half the size of their real chapel, for those people who stopped coming to church, or for new people who might want to join. It's an opportunity to meet new people and to have everyone pray that those who have left the church will return tonight, and will possibly even be saved. Days before, the deacons erected a prominent sign in the lawn of the church by the road which reads "HELL IS HOT". Angela is sure this alone will be enough to lure new members in.

The pastor and board of deacons of Forest Baptist Church had started planning this event almost a year earlier. They achieved quite a coup by getting *the* Brother

Jack Hyles to accept their humble invitation to speak to their congregation. Across the country, anybody's who's anybody in the conservative fundamentalist Baptist movement, from the loftiest preacher to the smallest born-again Christian child, knows that Brother Hyles is *the* Brother Hyles. Well known for his rich, smooth talk and brash fire and brimstone approach to salvation, he has spared thousands of souls from the depths of hell. He can melt skin off your bones with his mere words. Rumor has it that he speaks one-on-one with God every day. So, it is no surprise that the people under the white tent plan to hang on his every word tonight.

When Brother Hyles accepted the invitation to come and speak at their revival that autumn night, the congregation was elated—convinced they have contracted with the next best thing to Jesus. They have no doubt that souls will be saved at no expense and Satan will be defeated, yet again. All here in their little tent beside their own Forest Baptist Church.

Emotions run high among children and adults alike as Brother Hyles emerges from the back of the tent to a roaring applause. Angela can feel the electric charge in the air as everyone takes a seat and waits for the sounds of shifting chairs to settle under the weight of the crowd. Brother Hyles begins to speak to the congregation about why God has brought him to their church.

Angela tries to listen, but eventually gives in to distraction as her eyes grow heavy and her mind begins to wander upward through the seams of the tent into the night. She smells the night air outside the tent where there is an absence of cheap perfume and sweaty scents. She loves the feel of the evening, the soft, embracing breeze under the full moon and the faint songs of grasshoppers.

Suddenly, the thunderous voice of Brother Hyles who stands only inches in front of her, brings her back under the tent. "Ladies and Gentlemen, Satan is after your souls," he bellows. "He's after the souls of you and your loved ones! He is among us tonight, ready to strike at any moment!"

As if reading cue cards, the crowd yells a mixture of "Amen" and "Halleluiah" in response.

Angela glances behind her and scans the attentive audience. She wonders who among them are the un-saved. In her eight years in this movement, she is certain that virtually every member of the church and school has come forward. Brother Hyles will surely be disappointed that there is no one left for him to save. She worries that if no one comes forward, he may not return and she won't get the chance to worship outside again.

Angela spots her grandmother seated in the back next to all her aunts and uncles. Granny waves and Angela waves back, smiling at her family. She's happy they've all come tonight and thinks they look great in their fancy new clothes. Angela is sure that regardless of whether people come forward and are saved tonight, the evening will end at their favorite restaurant. She can almost taste her favorite dessert, blackberry cobbler.

As Brother Hyles' sermon lapses into a melodious stretch, the congregation braces themselves for the next unexpected outburst. They listen quietly as he calmly advises, "Satan comes to you through false prophets, soothsayers and temptation." He then leans forward and placing his hands on his knees, looks out over the congregation. He lowers his voice to slightly above a whisper and begins to share with the congregation a secret he has traveled all the way from Hammond, Indiana to tell.

"You see folks, we only get one chance. This is it. One chance to spare ourselves from eternal damnation," he says, lifting one finger in the air, pointing toward the heavens.

He straightens his back and returns to the pulpit where suddenly his eyebrows point downward, and with lips pressed together then opening widely, he angrily yells "I CAN HELP YOU ENTER HIS KINGDOM!" His fist lands with a loud thud on the cheaply constructed wooden pulpit. "Repent brothers and sisters! Drop to your knees and beg for mercy! We are all born in sin."

Brother Hyles's voice trembles as if in extreme pain and he begins to cry his next words in agony, targeting the children concentrated in the first two rows with his slow purposeful words. "You will burn in hell, your skin dripping . . . rotting . . . melting . . . from your bones." Recovering suddenly, he stands fully erect and bellows, "SAVE YOUR SOULS BEFORE IT'S TOO LATE!"

Though they have all been saved and should therefore have nothing to fear, the children in the front two rows collectively shrink back, cowering from the great preacher's words. The children have come to see this fear as a regular part of their lives. But Brother Hyles' unexpected outbursts are something new. His anger on their behalf seems misplaced. Surely he couldn't be speaking about them, as they have all been saved. The church believes in saving the children as soon as they can speak. Although the church rarely speaks about what happens to babies when they die, the general consensus among the churchgoers seems grim. Angela was told she was saved when she was only three years old, but she never remembered feeling any different. She was envious of her many friends who gave tearful testimonies of their own salvations, always to the delight of the adults who heard them. Angela wanted to be praised the way those children were praised. She wanted to remember. So, one day at school, she decided to get saved again, just to make sure. It was a memorable day for her and she was proud. When she came home and told her parents, they smiled and gave her a hug.

This happened on the day that Angela's kindergarten teacher, Mrs. Blaine, brought a large poster board divided in half by blue and red. Angela loved visuals, but even more than visuals, she loved teddy bears. Her teacher made teddy bears to go along with the poster board and demonstrated happy and sad bears. Happy bears were saved bears who went to heaven to live in big houses in the blue top portion of the poster board. Sad bears were not saved and were thrown into a lake of fire when they died. The teacher demonstrated the sad bears' descent into hell with the lower red portion of the poster board, a match and an ashtray.

Mrs. Blaine had every five-year old's attention as she explained how salvation worked. Much to the children's relief, one need only close their eyes and repeat a prayer and they would get to go to the blue portion of the poster board, live in big houses with happy bears and not burn. Angela was relieved it could be so easy.

She closed her eyes with her classmates and repeated after Mrs. Blaine, "Dear Jesus, please forgive me of my sins and save me. I believe you died on the cross for me, and I am now trusting in you to let me into heaven. Thank you for saving me. In Jesus' name Amen." Mrs. Blaine, smiling enthusiastically, took out a stack of little three by five "salvation" note cards from her desk. "Now children," she asked, "who here really meant what they said during that prayer?"

Angela, hoping to get a big house, shyly raised her hand with five other children. Mrs. Blaine then called them to the front of the class and made everyone else clap for them. It was a little embarrassing, but Angela knew she had done the right thing by admitting she didn't want to go to hell. Her other classmates were either still thinking about it, or already saved. The teacher told them all to pray for each other.

Mrs. Blaine completed the salvation note cards, which were forwarded to the church's office later in the day. Next Sunday, a small plaque holding numbers displayed in the front of the church's chapel would increase by five; five little souls had been given entrance into heaven. Everyone praised the Lord and thanked Mrs. Blaine for her soul-winning skills.

Back in the tent with Brother Hyles only a few feet away, Angela was relieved he was not speaking about her. She knew she would go to heaven if she could only behave. But she was concerned about her Daddy. A month ago, the preacher had said that people who don't go to church go to hell. Angela had cried for two days because even though she knew he believed in God, her Daddy had to work on Sundays. He couldn't even go to church during weeknights because he worked the graveyard shift at the airport nearby. Her mother tried to console her, but rules were rules and so they had to live with the idea that he might not go to heaven.

Luckily tonight, Angela's only preoccupation, shared with her friends, is avoiding being spit on by Brother Hyles who tends to expectorate when excited. With some words, small droplets of saliva would sail over the first two rows. Angela and the children hold their bibles tight, waiting for the moment when they would be called into action as shields to protect them. The bible-clutching that appeared to others as dedication and devotion among the children was actually just a form of self defense.

"Only the heavenly father can give you an eternal place in heaven! Our lives have already started to end. Hebrews 9:27 tells us all *'it's appointed unto men once to die, but after this . . . the judgment.'*"

He wipes the sweat from his brow with his surprisingly small hand, reaches for a drink of ice water with the other. Then, holding his tattered leather bible high in the air and motioning forward with his free hand, he proclaims, "God said *'And I give unto them eternal life; and they shall never perish'* . . . Get out of your seats ladies and gentleman, Come up here and save your souls!"

This is the organist's cue. A petite woman with long feathered hair, she looks around nervously, flings her hair onto her back and begins to play a small electric keyboard propped on a card table near the back of the stage. Everyone stands, bows heads and sings the hymn in solemn quiet tones while pretending not to peek at the sinners approaching the alter.

Have Thine own way, Lord. Have Thine own way
Thou art the Potter, I am the clay.
Mold me and make me after Thy will,
While I am waiting, yielded and still . . .

Angela lifts her head to sneak a peek as Brother Hyles wipes more sweat from his forehead. She sees him take off his black thick-rimmed glasses, squeeze his eyes together tightly, and clip the bridge of his nose with his fingers until tears escape from the outer corners of his eyes. The show is almost complete.

Brother Hyles begins to hum, then softly speaks while the congregation continues to sing.

"The Lord is my shepherd; I shall not want. He maketh me to lie down in green pastures: he leadeth me beside the still waters. Praise Jesus! *He restoreth my soul. . . ."*

Causes of Action

The morning air of Wednesday, April 23, 1919, feels crisp and refreshing. Fresh air flows through the open windows of a Queen and Crescent train headed north on the well-traveled line from the Queen city of Cincinnati to the Crescent city of New Orleans. The day before, the train had stopped in Lexington, Kentucky where a newlywed couple boarded the train accompanied by several guests.

Standing in a passageway of the train lined with windows, the new bride feels an unfamiliar freedom sweep over her as the warm morning breeze flows over her dressing gown in unison with the monotonous swaying of the train. The hypnotic clicking of the train's rails resonate through the train car as her mind fills with ideas and concerns that any new bride might have about the new life with her groom. She knows she has made a wise decision and married well, she just wishes her own family could support her more. Her family is large, and as she is not accustomed to being alone. She thinks of them and feels pangs of loneliness.

Her family, involved largely in the railroad industry, had reservations about the train's safety and begged her not to go. Their concerns were ridiculous to the new bride, who knew trains were nothing new. But sometimes her family frustrated her with their common and backward ways, she thought. She smiles kindly and tries not to think badly of them, as she knows they only act out of love for her.

Her husband's family is very different from her own, more refined, prominent and respected in the community. Her dedicated new groom is older than she and a serious business man. But, this morning, something else is on the new bride's mind. She feels sad and oddly betrayed as her husband has planned a business meeting this morning on the train, despite the fact it is their honeymoon.

These thoughts consume her as she looks out several partially opened windows where the wind playfully toys with the sheer cotton curtains. The windows are small and beautifully framed by well-crafted mahogany wood paneling. She turns her attention from the waving curtains to the long narrow passageway, feeling partially naked as the wind presses against her bare legs. Her new husband approaches and stands closely to her. He is slightly taller than she, in his thirties, with a rounded face and thinning hair. He is relaxed and only partially dressed, with his shirt slightly unbuttoned to reveal a large high collar appearing to stand on its own due to significant starching.

He has a knowing, almost sympathetic grin on his face as he looks at her with outreached hands. She softens immediately and her concerns fly out of her as easily as the wind passes through the train. He is a gentle, polite man. He anticipates her every need and can already read her mind with great ease. She loves him deeply and knows her future will be better because he will be a part of it. His manner is strong and direct yet loving. It is love at every sight, as it was at the first.

The groom leans towards his bride and whispers, "Don't worry my love, I won't be long. You know how important this is to me. I will return for you very shortly." Placing both hands on her shoulders, he presses her gently back against the wall, raises one hand to her cheek, and slowly lowers his head to kiss her. Feelings of warmth and tenderness flow through their bodies as they feel their souls embrace. It's a love few have the privilege of experiencing once in a lifetime, yet alone twice.

The scene changes suddenly and the new bride finds herself in a lavishly decorated parlor. She is no longer on the train. "Come in dear. Have a seat," says her groom's aunt who is seated regally in a high back chair upholstered in lush burgundy velvet. The aunt motions to the seat in front of her. She is overweight, but poised, with impeccable grooming. Her makeup is heavily applied and her hair is neatly placed on top of her head. "Lilly, could you please bring us some tea?" the aunt asks of the diminutive young woman patiently waiting at the door behind the new bride. The new bride is proud to be in her company, as she knows the aunt is the finest example of a successful socialite of her time.

"Yes Ma'am. Right away," a voice behind the bride sounds.

The new bride is taken in by the beauty and richness of the décor and is immediately filled with a sense of gratitude and respect. "Thank you for having me," the bride says shyly as she takes a seat in front of her new aunt.

"How are you dear? Are you finding the adjustment difficult with your age?" she asks. The new bride smiles and thinks to herself that she is probably being overbearing and childish about her husband's absences, but she feels insecure about her new role as wife, taken on so late in her life, when others have already labeled her a spinster.

"Actually . . . yes. It has been difficult. He works a lot. I guess I wasn't prepared for that. He even left me to do work on our honeymoon! On the train! I was shocked to say the least. He knew I was upset but he went anyway. Do you think I overreacted? Was it wrong of me to get so upset with him?"

A kind grin spreads across the aunt's soft, plump face as she says, "No. But there are things you must now understand and remember. I know the adjustment will be difficult. Right now, you don't want him out of your sight one minute. But, that will all change."

She stops to take her tea from Lilly, elegantly served in a fine white china teacup and saucer with small pink roses trimmed in gold. "You must understand that your husband's business is your business. He will take care of it and it will take care of you and your family. You must concentrate on making a family and a happy home. He has a job to do, but so do you". She grins at the new bride as she takes her tea.

The scene changes again and the new bride is back on the train. A warm glowing light emanates from a hidden source, casting a haze down a dimly lit corridor. The new bride makes a right turn into another room where she notices a large oval gold leaf mirror on the wall. Inside the mirror is a stranger looking back at her. The stranger appears to be in her mid-twenties and is wearing the same thin cotton white gown as the new bride. The stranger moves her arm in unison with the new bride's, running her hand along the exposed shoulder bones that hold up her small narrow frame. The stranger's hair is dark, straight and long, as is the bride's. The bride knows that it is time for them both to go to bed.

It's seven o'clock in the morning and Angela is sleeping soundly when the alarm clock shatters her peace. Awakening in a panic, she gropes with her left arm desperately in search of the painful noise. Angela's eyes are slow to open and her body reluctant to ease out of its nocturnal state. Her left arm finally hits its target and finds the correct button that will stop the hideous noise. This is not an uncommon ritual of Angela's morning, but this time, the alarm clock's assault is particularly brutal and calls for more extreme action. This time, her left arm does something extra: It hurls her alarm clock across the room towards the trash can, missing by only inches.

All the commotion wakes up her husband of five years, lying next to her. "What was all that about?" Brent asks, half asleep.

"I hate alarm clocks. They are so unnatural!" she complains as she gets out of bed and stumbles over her dog who is seemingly unmoved by the loud noises and flying objects. "Who the hell invented such a horrible contraption? All they do is interrupt perfectly good dreams and keep us from working out perfectly good scenarios in our minds, which in turn causes us to be grumpy all day!" Angela complains.

"So now that you threw it away you won't be grumpy?" her husband asks, teasing her with his strong British accent, as she heads to the bathroom.

"Ha, Ha. Funny. For your information, I was having a perfectly wonderful honeymoon with an amazing man on a beautiful train. Except I was tall, skinny, rather plain looking and I wasn't married to you!" Angela sticks out her tongue and then turns from him to start the shower. "And, since we never had a honeymoon . . . it certainly wasn't ours," Angela says firmly as she takes off her nightgown, throws it forcefully in the floor and gets in the shower.

"You really need to get over not having a honeymoon," her husband yells from across the room.

"You know I don't care about that. Who needs one when I can have one just as real in my dreams?" she says in a calmer tone. A more pensive mood is settling in as she starts to remember her dream. Each aspect of the dream permeates her skin as the flowing water of the shower envelopes and purifies her body. Angela finishes the shower, dries her hair, steps into a suit, applies her makeup and stands before her floor length mirror before leaving for work. She stares at her image, raises her hand to her collarbones and mimics herself from the dream. It's no wonder women have a hard time accepting their bodies. Less than an hour ago, Angela was a taller, slimmer brunette newlywed on a train. Now, awake and completely in the present, she occupies a short body with rounded hips, pale white skin with freckles and blonde hair. The contrast feels almost abrupt as puberty, when Angela's change in outward appearance ushered in a completely new environment and changed her life forever.

The woman in the mirror before her, dressed in a short-skirted professional designer suit and black hose has come a long way from the Christian school girl with demure long skirts and saddle oxfords. Angela looks over at the clothes hanging in her closet next to the mirror and remembers spending most of her childhood mornings in the Christian school, standing in line with other girls waiting to get on her knees to have their skirts measured with a ruler. The wardrobe hanging before her now is a declaration of freedom, and her obsession with fine, modern clothing a silent act of rebellion. As a pre-teen, she resented the Church's strict rules on her growing body and couldn't understand their obsession with her changing outward appearance.

Angela, now all grown up, thinks back on these events as she moves back to the mirror and whispers grudgingly, "What sickos. The line between holiness and whoredom in pre-teen girls did not lie somewhere within an inch of our knees."

The pantsuits hanging in Angela's closet are her greatest symbol of freedom from her past. She was not allowed to wear pants to school or at home, at any age. This rule was imposed by the school, not by her parents, especially not her mother who freely wore pants despite the church's teachings. Every start of the school year began with the ritual of "the pledge", or "plague" as the students secretly called it. The pledge was a contract the school required every student to sign. It spelled out the rules of Christian behavior and required students to comport themselves in accordance at all times. Rules included not listening to rock music or music scores containing drum beats, which were considered the "devil's beat". Visits to movie theaters were prohibited. The children were confined to the school's dress code away from school, maintaining a Christian appearance at all times. This meant no pants or shorts for the girls, while boys need only maintain their short hair. Church attendance and soul winning were also expected.

Students would line the pews in the spacious chapel and take their seats when the church's pastor entered and stood in front of the baptismal filled with lime green water, set above the stage behind the choir loft. The school's secretarial staff would come with stacks of paper and hand them to the children on the outside of the rows to pass down. A prayer was said, the significance of a promise discussed, and everyone was told to sign the contracts with God. If they didn't, they would not be allowed to continue at the school. The children were in a precarious position, as very few would have chosen to go to this school had they been able to exercise their God-given free will. The choice was their parent's, and now they were forced to sign away something they never had to begin with.

The "plague" requirement began as soon as the children reached seventh grade, as soon as Angela grew breasts and began her period. She realized that everything that was making her a woman was hated by her religion. She was no longer a beautiful child, the reflection of God's love. She became a woman, an object of temptation which would lure the men to damned ground much like Eve did for Adam. She would have to be cautious in her dress, attitude and comportment. And so, at the tender age of eleven, Angela boldly fantasized about breaking out into the great world one day wearing pants or a mini skirt and making something of herself besides a preacher's wife or missionary. The closet before her now was proof she had achieved that goal.

When Angela unexpectedly left the school and church after a series of events when she was thirteen, she threw herself into her education, the one thing her parents promised would never let her down, and she never looked back. The change was refreshing and addictive. Angela's interests moved far from where she had been. She studied foreign languages, majored in international studies in college and became a foreign exchange student more than once, spending her last summer of college in England.

It was there that Angela met Brent Salinger. They fell in love while she was attending Oxford University on a full scholarship to study international relations. Brent was not far from his home in Kidlington and was in his last year at Oxford, majoring in English literature.

They had met unexpectedly in the university's library after Angela fell down a flight of stairs. Her fall was quite dramatic due to the echo quality of the old architecture. She landed on her back, legs in the air, surrounded by books. Brent was behind her and witnessed with horror the entire event. He was sure she had broken every bone in her body and was prepared to carry her small body the rest of the way down the stairs just as she started howling with laughter. Her laughter was contagious and soon Brent was helping her up to stand on her own two feet and falling in love.

Angela loved Brent's strong British accent. He always sounded so formal and educated—a far cry from the sounds she was accustomed to. He loved her southern drawl. Angela, could not conceal her accent no matter how hard she tried. She thought it made her sound stupid and flirty. He thought it made her sound genuine and sweet.

Their romance was brief, but its impact undeniable. It seemed to be a trend for Angela, this falling madly in love with men she could not have. Geographic distance was the evil that had destroyed previous attempts at love. The trend manifested itself early in her life, when, at the young age of fourteen, after Angela's best friend moved to California, she visited her. She fell madly in love with her best friend's neighbor,

Aaron. The feeling was mutual and through the years they kept in touch though they never saw each other again. They eventually had to settle for friendship.

Six years after Aaron, came Victor, a gorgeous brown haired, muscle-bound New York native. He was also a neighbor of one of her friends. They met accidentally on the phone, each completely enthralled with the other's voice from the first conversation. Their relationship and phone bills grew until they could resist no longer. He finally came to Georgia to visit her, and their whirlwind romance knocked her off her feet. She fell madly in love with him and cried inconsolably for weeks when he decided to join the Peace Corps, move to Uganda and save the world.

She swore she would never cry in another airport over any man but wasn't able to keep her promise as she boarded her flight back for her senior year of college in the States. Angela had endured so many long distance relationships before meeting Brent that she couldn't bear the pain and torture of another. She was now convinced she would forever be cursed to love faraway people. So, with a tearstained face and daggers in her heart, she told him it was over and that he should find someone new.

One and a half years later, Angela and Brent were married in a small non-denominational chapel on her university's campus. Soon thereafter, they moved together to Miami so that Angela could attend law school. Brent worked hard in odd jobs in the hotel industry to support them through those difficult years. Angela promised in return to support him after graduation while he worked on his Ph.D. in English literature at Emory University, her alma mater in her hometown of Atlanta. She always kept her promises.

Most days, Angela finds it hard to believe she's an attorney. Always very driven as a child, she knew she'd have a career someday, but now at 28, she wonders where all the excitement is. Attending the best private colleges and universities earned her a bachelor's degree, a doctor of law degree, and a pile of student loans in exchange for the hopes of living an interesting life filled with meetings, international travel and important things to do to help others. Instead, she has found unhappy people with problems bigger than their faith, commonly filled with a need for revenge. As an attorney, she sells packages of revenge, filled with law suits and nasty letters on firm letterhead meant to scare adversaries into submission. She learned not to meet her client's adversaries face to face early on. She did better with calls, letters and pleadings. Once they saw her tiny five-foot stature, unassuming voice and blonde hair, they wouldn't take her seriously.

But the firm of Petrowski, Morgan and Kline, a small firm in downtown Atlanta, took a chance with her. Impressed with her education and study abroad experiences, they hired her fresh out of law school four years ago, even though they had nothing "international" or exciting to offer. Angela knew they had sensed the faint smell of desperation and hunger hanging on her borrowed interview suit, but she was glad to have a job, as she knew student loans would soon come due. She quickly made a name for herself and gained the respect of others by working behind the scenes on the firm's cases that went to court. One partner refers to her as the "fighting Fifi" of the firm, outwardly, sweet and cuddly, but cross her in any way and she'll bite. She hated this degrading comparison, and struggled to accept it as the compliment she longed for every time it was muttered.

The cases ranged from the occasional commercial leases to corporate law suits and wrongful termination cases. Each case had its own identity, but after four years of seeing the same kinds of cases and disputes over and over again, it was easy to get confused. Whenever she had a meeting with a new potential client, she could almost recount their tearful stories verbatim before they sat uncomfortably before her desk. She had heard it all before. Some just wanted help with their businesses. Others wanted revenge. For the right price, Angela could deliver both.

When Angela arrives at work the morning after her dream, she is greeted by a stack of yesterday's sorted mail regarding her cases, along with voicemails and emails awaiting a response. Angela takes a deep breath and decides which of the three sets of chores she will tackle first. Voicemail wins out. It's a good morning— only seven voicemails in the queue, three of which are from her mom.

"Hi Hon. I don't know if you're at work yet, but I wanted to remind you about my doctor's appointment today. Call me back when you get this message . . ."

"Hey, it's me again. I was just thinking you should probably be at my house by about 1:00 just in case there's a lot of traffic . . ."

"Well, it's 9:30 and I haven't heard from you. Call me as soon as you get in . . ."

Angela's mother is one of the few people Angela will actually listen to, despite her tendency to chop up one simple thought into a bunch of voicemail messages. An incredibly strong woman with horrible luck, Angela's mother Brenda always manages to pull through each life tragedy with a smile on her face. Angela is dragged along with her from one tragedy to another, but would not have it any other way. She loves her mother dearly.

Most of the tragedies they got through together in the past had to do with her mother's health. Sometimes, it was chronic illnesses, such as asthma. Other times, it was something to do with her vision. Today however, a newly diagnosed fractured spine is on the agenda, and what seems like a frightening complication to most is just life as usual for Angela and her mom.

Angela leaves work soon after lunch, essentially abandoning a new client in the waiting room. Her partner knew she had to take her mother to the doctor, but had insisted on making the appointment anyway. Angela's response to him is one he has came to expect from his strong minded, determined associate "I'm sorry Mr. Kline. You've known for two weeks that I had this appointment, and I reminded you two days ago and then again yesterday but you made the appointment anyway. You created this problem for yourself," she says unsympathetically as she storms out the front door.

Angela almost hopes Mr. Kline will fire her. She half suspects that his deliberate attempt to interfere with her personal business during the workday is sabotage that will give him an excuse to fire her. He wouldn't fire her though, at least not on this day. He thinks she's cute and loves her innocent appearance and little black shoes.

Angela fights her way south out of the congested Atlanta streets to her mother's house. Her mother and father live in the same two-bedroom ranch-style brick home Angela grew up in. Because her father travels often with his recent career move in the travel industry,

Angela is more commonly the caretaker of her mother. Even though it is normally only a thirty-minute drive south of Atlanta, the trip takes Angela almost an hour today. When Angela arrives, her mother is still in the bedroom trying to get dressed.

"Well, I've got one leg in and two arms covered" Brenda says, laughing as she tries to balance herself on the side of the bed while leaning unnaturally to her left.

"Your back must be killing you like this, Mom! Here, let me get this" Angela offers while reaching down to help her finish getting dressed.

Brenda puts all her weight on her daughter to keep from falling. Her short, plump legs are numb and no matter how she stands, every step triggers a sharp pain in her back. Her cotton sleeve has twisted and wrapped around her right arm. Her left wrist and hand hang use-lessly as she struggles to move her fingers, which lost their dexterity after a fall crushed her wrist a year ago. Angela carefully adjusts the sleeves and pulls the other pant leg up her mother's leg. Brenda, blind in one eye, has also put on mismatched socks, which Angela takes off and patiently replaces with matching white socks from the bottom of her disorganized sock drawer. With every movement, Angela can sense her mother's pain scaling up her back and around her waist with every move.

Anticipating her mother's physical difficulties, Angela had parked her car on the front lawn, lining up the passenger door with the front door of the house. "I hope you didn't run over Ms. Betty's flowers!" her mom says disapprovingly as she glares at the car sitting in her front yard.

"Don't worry, I didn't . . . but your petunias gave the ultimate sacrifice as I rolled over them," Angela says without hiding her delight. "Would you have preferred to walk down the driveway to my car?"

Brenda smiles, shakes her head and climbs into the front seat of Angela's car, knowing she is no match for her daughter's sharp wit. It would be a long ride to the doctor's office today. Getting from one place to another was the most difficult part of traveling with her mother and the fractured spine. They ride along in relative silence, both contemplating the upcoming logistics of getting in and out of the doctor's office.

Brenda is the first to break the silence. "You know, whenever I get to feeling better, we should start going to church again."

"Mom. We've had this conversation a thousand times and the answer is NO. I am not going to church with you or Daddy or the entire family."

"But this new church is so different. Your Aunt Lillian likes it, and some of your cousins visited and liked it too."

"You know all churches make me want to throw up, Mom." Angela says, rolling her eyes.

"But they're so different from Forest Baptist. They're really liberal. Why, some of the ladies even wear pants to church! And, they let you read and study any bible, not just the King James Version. And they have some really upbeat music before the sermons begin. I think you would like it."

"Does the sign out front say 'Baptist'?" Angela asks.

"Yes."

"Then I'm not going."

Brenda takes a deep breath, looks over at her stubborn daughter and begins, "you need to get over Forest Baptist. It happened a long time ago and it wouldn't be a bad thing to get back into church. Forest

Baptist was a fundamental independent Baptist church, not like the liberal mainstream Southern Baptist."

"Mainstream liberal Southern Baptist?" Angela interrupts. "You have got to be kidding, Mom! Nothing about Southern Baptist screams mainstream or liberal to me. I don't care how different Forest Baptist is from this new church or other Baptist churches. The sign out front read Baptist, not independent-fundamental-not-mainstream-southern-Baptist. All I knew growing up was that I was Christian and Baptist . . . I'm just not interested.

"Mom, do you know that I actually have anxiety attacks when I walk into a church? I can barely get through the lobby and into the pews without a nauseous wave coming over me and breaking out in cold sweats. That's not good, Mother. Something is wrong there. And honestly, I don't worship the same mean vengeful god they believe in anyway. It's better if I stay away, because I have my own ideas and I can't be nice or respectful."

Brenda looks out her passenger window frustrated with her daughter, grimacing from the pain streaking through her body. "I'm so sorry I kept you in that school," she says with regret. "If your father and I had known what all was really going on with them or you, we wouldn't have made you stay. But we believed you were getting a really good education, better than any public school in Georgia could've offered."

"I did get a great education, but, Mom, I told you what was going on," says Angela, glancing over at Brenda in disbelief.

"I know. But your father and I thought you were exaggerating . . . We didn't think they were really measuring your skirts or spanking y'all so much," sighs Brenda.

"Well," Angela sighs, "I left and it's in the past. I'm not sure I'll ever recover from all of that, but that is my problem to deal with, not yours or Daddy's ok? I reject organized religion to stay safe. It's my personal religious choice."

"Ok dear. Just remind me of that from time to time, okay?"

"Don't worry, Mom, you know I will."

Honesty, the one thing Angela valued most, was the one value that broke the foundation of her religious upbringing. Her quest for truth in everything made her hypersensitive to the hypocrisy she slowly realized was all around her. Strict legalistic interpretations taught to her since birth began to backfire.

Something as simple as a community garage sale in the church's parking lot sparked a spiritual crisis in Angela. "How could they do such a thing?" she wondered in shocked disbelief, recalling the only time in the bible Jesus was actually violent was when merchants were selling things outside the church. Her questions went unanswered, or worse, punished.

School was no different, as the teachings were all the same. One day in bible class her teacher casually mentioned that God had turned water into grape juice, not wine, as it is written. Angela was floored. "But how can it be wrong? We've been taught the bible is flawless and the Word of God?" she asked, sure the teacher was mistaken.

"It was a translation error" her teacher informed. It was more serious than Angela had calculated and before she could control her tongue she innocently asked out loud, "so how do we know they got the Ten Commandments right?"

Angela didn't wait for an answer. Instead, she

closed her eyes tight, realizing her thoughts had once again slipped out of her weak lips.

"Blasphemy!" her teacher cried, as Angela was sent to the end of the hall to await her paddling. Slowly, in situations such as these, the comforting, embracing fog surrounding who the teachers and church leaders really were was lifting. Angela could see them for the meanness they had become, or had always been. Their reputations in the church became much more important than their reputations before their God. When their children slowly began to think on their own and question, they'd shake their heads and beg with prayers that God should show them their way. Their children became the pitiful reflections of all they hated and feared. All the while, droplets of the adults' own hypocrisy were washing away the faith of the children. They never even noticed.

"So, how was your day going before I brought up this touchy subject?" Brenda asks, trying to initiate normal conversation.

"Well, work is work. Brent had to go to the library early this morning . . . And, I had another one of those dreams last night."

"Really? Which dream was that?"

"That honeymoon dream. Didn't I tell you about it before? The one that seems so real. The one where I'm on the train and my husband ditches me to go off to some business meeting. I've probably had that dream about four times now," Angela explains as she turns into the parking lot of the doctor's office.

"You mentioned something about it, but I thought it was the same honeymoon dream you used to have when you were little."

At that moment, Angela feels a sinking sensation

in her stomach. "Oh my God, Mom! You're right!" Angela was amazed and excited all at once. "I used to have a honeymoon dream when I was little. . . . This one is different though. . . . I can't believe you remembered that! It's as clear as yesterday too. . . . We were in a hotel." She looks at her mother with a hint of terror in her eyes, "I wonder if they are related?"

"No . . ." Brenda replies. "How could they be? You weren't much older than seven when you had those dreams over and over. You were probably just having some kind of obsession with honeymoons," laughs her mother. Angela wasn't laughing. She wished her mother were right, but she suspected she wasn't. Angela wasn't a romantic, and certainly didn't care about honeymoons.

She came to call it her honeymoon dream. The beginning was always the same. Angela, just a seven year old is grown up in her dream. She's in a beautiful hotel walking down a corridor with arched ceilings, not unlike a ceiling you would find in a cathedral. She is happy and content with her new status as a married woman. As she gazes up at the beautiful ceiling and down the opulent corridor, she can hear the faint sounds of a man's voice. She doesn't care much about what the man has to say, she only wants to absorb the architectural beauty and savor the moment. Her right hand is securely wrapped around her new husband's left arm as they stroll down the corridor. On his right is the man she doesn't care to listen to.

He is an important person at this hotel. He is giving Angela and her new husband a private tour. Her husband's family has arranged the private tour, as they are in the hotel business. Angela and her groom have the distinct pleasure of being treated as VIPs for the evening. But, their evening comes to an abrupt end when a fire alarm sounds. Angela is then separated from her groom and finds herself very concerned about something left in their hotel room's closet.

When little Angela awakens from this dream, she always has the same feeling. She says to herself time and time again, "Oh, that dream again. I like that dream". She feels gratitude for being treated as an important person and pride walking alongside her husband, for whom she genuinely feels love . . . even as a seven year old. She is not affected by the fire alarm, nor does she sense she is in any immediate danger. Until now, she considered it just another little girl's dream of being a grown-up.

The Century Turns

O nce a routine is practiced, the ancient art of yoga becomes graceful, rhythmic and soothing. Mind, body and spirit join together to complement each other in the ultimate dance between physical and mental realms. The threads that unite the body with the mind are exposed. And like a puppeteer, the spirit takes over to dominate a restless, uncontrolled body.

Yoga, literally meaning a "union of the body, mind and spirit" derived from its Sanskrit root, dates back to ancient civilizations but has been practiced in the United States only since the 1800s. Yoga in and of itself is not a religion. But, many religions and cultures claim yoga as an integral part of their spiritual well being, much like western religions embrace the common theme of prayer. Actually, to someone actively practicing both yoga and prayer, the distinction can become quite blurred.

When Angela began to practice yoga a year ago, it was purely for relaxation and stress relief. She was determined to ward off the stressful side effects of her profession and taking care of her disabled mother. To her surprise, she quickly found she was really good at it. She enjoyed the stretching and challenging poses of yoga. But, she found that her favorite part of yoga was towards the end, when she could lie like a downed tree, plant her roots, empty her mind and meditate. She loved this form of meditation where only her mind and the music were present. She could feel her body melt into the mat and lose all touch with reality. It was addictive.

Angela learned the moves and exercises at a yoga center close to her home. She had advanced to the intermediate level, which meant she could do most of the poses without falling over, hurting herself, or laughing hysterically. The center was in a small house, with its rooms converted into small studios for classes. Angela loved the atmosphere. She felt relaxed as soon as she opened the front door and saw the people who were always so friendly. They were people she would see at the park, the pharmacy, or her local grocery store. She marveled at the simplicity of the décor and wondered if it would ever be possible for her to turn her own office at the formal, stiff law firm into a relaxing and inviting place. She would much rather be here, going through yoga moves, stretching her body and feeling her muscles tone, relax and build strength.

Angela's yoga teacher, Fred, lightly touches her shoulder to inform her that class is over. Angela is still meditating, spread eagle on the floor, oblivious to everyone walking around her, gathering their belongings and whispering. She comes out of her meditation and, irritated, looks around. "Fred, why don't you give us more time to meditate?" she asks.

All six and a half feet of Fred tower over Angela as she lies motionless on a mat. "You had fifteen minutes! How much more do you need, woman?"

Angela lifts her heavy arm over her head and exclaims, "No way! There's no way that was fifteen minutes. It felt more like five minutes to me!"

"If you want to lie around and meditate all night, you should consider the meditation class Savannah teaches on Saturdays. They're starting up a class this week, so I bet it's not too late to sign up. Ask Raven about it if you're interested." He says kindly.

While Angela can always rationalize taking yoga as a necessary part of health and exercise, a structured meditation course is altogether different. She's not sure she's ready to take that next step as she looks up at Fred, still trying to fully wake up. All the weirdos take the meditation classes, those seeking some form of enlightenment not otherwise provided by their normal, completely boring lives. And, Angela thinks, there is sometimes a religious aspect to meditation, which she wants no part of.

Images of little monks meditating on platforms with blissful stares on their faces alternate in her mind with scenes of hippies seated in the lotus position surrounded by incense and daisies. No, she can have no part in a meditation class. It just doesn't appeal to her.

"No. I don't think that's for me, Fred." Angela says.

"Don't be ridiculous," he responds, stopping before the classroom door. "If you like it so much you should give it a try."

Perhaps he's right. She did enjoy it. She doesn't do it for religious reasons. It's just the end part of her yoga routine. Maybe she should give it a try. She promises herself that if any hippies or funny looking incense salesmen show up, she will leave.

"Okay, okay. I will," Angela says slowly as she gets up and gathers her things.

At the front desk, Raven is busy filling out forms

and chewing organic gum. Angela places her gym bag and coat to the side and peers over the reception desk to catch Raven's attention. "Raven, I was wondering if there's any room left in the new meditation class starting up on Saturday morning?" she asks.

"Sure. I'll put you on the list. It's a promotional rate since you're already in a yoga class. It's $25 for the entire course." Angela hands her the money and promises to return on time Saturday morning.

Arriving the next Saturday for class, Angela is pleased to see a rather "normal" crowd—normal in the not-what-one-would-expect-of-hard-core-meditators kind of way. She doesn't spot any Birkenstocks, flowers in braided hair or long dresses—men included. There is also no incense salesperson lurking in the lobby when she arrives. To her relief, her classmates have on comfortable clothes suitable for the occasion, but, just as with her yoga classmates, they could easily be Angela's neighbors or co-workers.

The group stands around nervously while their instructor, Savannah, prepares and assigns cushions for each of the students. "Okay, everyone. Make friends with a cushion and stand in front of it!" she calls out to the students who are awaiting their first direction.

Savannah is more in touch with the image Angela has of what someone who meditates looks like. She has long, straight, dry brown hair, no make-up on her 40-plus year old face, toes spilling over the end of flip flops, and a pink and purple leotard two sizes too large.

"Now . . . everyone root yourselves on your cushions," she instructs in a wistful tone. Some students sit down, but the man standing next to Angela looks confused. "How do we do that?" he asks Angela. Angela giggles and kindly whispers over to him. "I think that's meditation talk for sit down". The man laughs along with her and, embarrassed, clumsily lowers himself onto his cushion beside her. Angela finds his sense of humor and insecurity refreshing, as she is sure at least one other person will probably do worse than her.

Savannah then starts explaining the different kinds of yoga and meditation. Angela recognizes most of the students from past yoga classes, but sees quite a few new people she has never seen before. They all have very serious expressions on their faces, and it is all Angela can do to keep from laughing. She realizes that while she is there to relax, others are there to learn how to relax. She always thought before that her ability to relax was just laziness. She's confident she will do well with group meditation.

"Okay," the instructor says in an excited whisper. "Now, everyone start by straightening your spines. Place your hands on your knees palm open, and touch your forefinger to your thumb. Feel your muscles relaxing as you quiet your mind. Let your busy thoughts float away and concentrate on your body relaxing. Feel your eyes descend behind your cheeks as you feel the weight of your body slowly dissipate.

"Now that you are completely relaxed, I want everyone, in unison, to chant 'Ommmmmm' as long as you can." The class does as they are instructed, including Angela. She relaxes easily and begins to concentrate on her "Omm". She opens one eye and glances around the room. Everyone appears to be getting the hang of it, but when Angela centers herself again and returns to the meditation she starts to feel very uncomfortable. It's as if she can actually feel the vibration of the collective 'mmmmm' throughout her body, flowing at her in waves. It is not the pleasant sensation she was expecting. She stops. "Wait. I can't do this," she says out loud, interrupting everyone's meditation.

Savannah is patient. "It's okay. Sometimes it takes people some time to get the hang of it. You're just a beginner. Concentrate and let yourself go . . . You'll learn."

"No. You don't understand. I'm feeling sick at my stomach," Angela advises with her voice lowered. Others close their eyes again and continue making their sounds.

"You're probably not completely relaxed. Take a minute and then join us when you're ready". The instructor then returns to her meditation and Ommming.

Angela, accustomed to excelling in classrooms, is disappointed that she has interrupted her class. She worries that she might be a complete failure at meditation. Determined to make it work, she closes her eyes once again, this time without saying the requisite "Ommm". She centers herself on her cushion, relaxes her body and feels the fibers of her face release. She can hear the others making their sounds and decides to give it another try. She begins to say "Ommm" again with the group.

Suddenly, and without warning, she feels an enormous wave of vibration run through her body, settling in her throat making her nauseous and dizzy. She feels as though her body is taking on all the vibration coming out of the mouths of her classmates. Their sounds attack her, throwing her off balance. She is certain that at any moment the man seated next to her in a blissful meditative trance will be covered in vomit.

Instead of interrupting the class, she runs out the back door straight to the bathroom, making it just in time. Angela decides this kind of torturous meditation is not for her and heads to the front desk to attempt to explain her predicament. Raven happily refunds her money and Angela returns home in complete resignation of her failure at meditation.

She reassures herself during the drive home, thinking, "I prefer the kind of meditation that doesn't make you look like an idiot anyway. I like the spread eagle flat on my back approach with soothing music from a yoga video tape in the privacy of my own home." At home, there is nobody to tell Angela it is time to get up. She can meditate as long as she can avoid falling sleep. She never feels sick at home. And, if it has anything to do with religion, she prefers to be alone in the safety of her own home.

When Angela arrives home, she finds a note from Brent saying he has classes until late that night. This will mean she'll have the house to herself, except of course for the dog. Her dog, Baghi, a black Labrador, greets her at the door wagging his tail and frisking her for treats. She gives him a few and then sets out for the bedroom to change from her loose sweat suit into her yoga clothes. She stretches the material over her head, pets Baghi's back and then bounces down the stairs.

Once downstairs, she puts in her favorite yoga tape and makes her way through the poses. As the tape nears its end, Angela is relieved. She is exhausted and looking forward to the meditation portion. The tape begins the soothing sounds Angela always looks forward to hearing. The instructor on the tape lulls her into complete relaxation, leaving nothing but soothing music flowing around her.

Without any prompting, Angela imagines a soothing white light surrounding and warming her, relaxing every molecule in her body. She feels her body slowly melt into the floor of her living room as the weight of her muscles surrender to complete and total relaxation.

A slight numbness travels across her face resembling a veil being softly lifted, dragged across her cheek, and onto the floor. She knows she is now free to travel the depths of her imagination. Her mind and spirit take a moment to breathe.

Suddenly, the music becomes faint and Angela is no longer aware of her body. "How strange," she thinks, "and how wonderful." She soon realizes that she is walking down a sidewalk in a city. Looking down at her left hand, she sees that she is wearing a crisp, white glove with a delicate small white bag dangling from the wrist with a ribbon-like handle. Her hand opens and there are two large shiny gold coins in the palm. The sun's reflection on the oversized coins temporarily blinds her as she thinks to herself, "This is a lot of money. I should put it in my purse."

Her attention is then drawn to her wrist. The sleeve to her white dress has a beautiful, delicate sky blue lace trim at the wrist. "I did a pretty good job on the trim to this dress," she says to herself, smiling at her handiwork while continuing to walk. She has put on her best clothes to go to town. She is going to buy shoes. Her favorite shoe store is up the block just a little way on her left.

She looks up ahead of her and sees that she is walking along the left side of the town on a sidewalk. People are crossing back and forth and down the middle of the street. Ladies are dressed in hats and colorful turn of the century long dresses. Angela notices two ladies walking side by side, crossing the street. One is dressed in a long ankle-length bright green dress with a large brim hat decorated with pleated ribbons and matching lace. She talks continuously as her friend, dressed in bright pumpkin orange, listens intently. Angela is repulsed by the eye straining combination of the two boldly colored gowns and stops, even though she feels her body continuing to walk towards the shoe store. "How odd" she thinks, staring at the brightly colored dresses. "This is nothing like the movies." There are virtually no dresses in the dull blues, browns and grays you commonly see on the big screen. She glances up and looks at the city. The buildings she passes are short and boxy. None appears to be over four stories. She is walking towards the edge of the city. There is no intersection; the street seems to end into nothing.

The scene changes and she is at the shoe store, lacing up a pair of pumps on a stool, a large display window to her right. The dim store of the light glistens off the new shoes as ladies and gentlemen pass by the storefront window outside. She carefully covers her leg with her long dress, safeguarding her modest reputation.

She is then horrified as she feels something wet on her face. It's a large tongue! She slowly opens her eyes to see Baghi staring at her nose-to-nose. Angela sits up, shakes her head a little bit, stretches, and tries to orient herself. The tape has completed, rewound itself and is perched halfway out of the VCR. "I must have been out for quite some time," she thinks to herself. She sits in silence amazed by the dream. Everything was so crisp, clear and real. She could sense everything—feel the heat, even smell. She imagines that there are few dreams in a lifetime that allow one to actually smell. Once you have one, you certainly won't forget it. She senses the realness of the dream without fear and actually laughs to herself about the colorful dresses crossing the street. "Wouldn't Hollywood be disappointed to know they have the costumes all wrong?" she says to her dog, panting over her. "Probably not," she concludes. She gets up, walks to the kitchen and drinks an entire glass of water.

The Harper family is blessed with their ancestors' good fortune in the Georgia marble business. Their account is considered the largest client at the law firm where Angela works. But, as is often the case, common sense and good business ethics do not always pass down through the generations. The remaining Harper heirs consist almost entirely of greedy, selfish, self-centered, materialistic whiners, or at least that's how Angela sees them. Even though she despises these characteristics, she knows they lend security to her paycheck at the firm.

Carl Prinston, the firm's lead litigator, had handled the Harper accounts for more than twenty-five years. Any dispute or problem the family has had passed through Carl. He is a ruthless but efficient attorney—a key asset to the firm. When Carl was diagnosed with cancer, it was as if the entire firm had been diagnosed as well. Everyone felt sick and worried about the future. They worried about making enough money to send their children to private schools, pay for their new cars, and keep up their young girlfriends. Angela worried about keeping her job and paying her student loan bills. They all wished Carl well, from the bottom of their hearts and checking accounts.

Mr. Petrowski, the firm's managing partner, called a meeting with all of the partners and associates as soon as word began to spread about Carl's condition. Everyone was afraid to go to the meeting, including Angela, for fear that Mr. Petrowski would announce Carl had decided to leave the practice, or worse, had died. Luckily, neither situation was the case. The attorneys file into the conference room decorated in faded peach wallpaper and artificial flowers. Each takes the same chairs they always take around the oval meeting table. Mr. Petrowski, seated at the head, stands up and announces "I'm sorry for the short notice about the meeting. As we all know, Carl is ill and will be out on extended leave for a time. We don't know how long."

The room becomes completely silent, each attorney hanging on his every word. "We have to distribute his cases, and I'm asking everyone to help out during this difficult time that I hope will not last too long." He picks up his clipboard and shuffles some of the pages. "Carl has a few open cases, including the Noytec account that is approaching trial. John, since you've been counsel with him throughout discovery, I naturally expect you to continue with the case, soliciting help from others in the firm as you see fit." John nods in agreement, secretly thrilled cancer is consuming his rival. Mr. Petrowski now turns his attention to Angela. "Angela, I want you to take charge on any new matters that may come up with the Harpers. I don't have to remind you how important they are to this firm," he says.

"Of course not. I'll handle it. Thank you," Angela responds.

"There is nothing pending right now, but I hear sweet Mitzie is planning a wedding. So we're counting on getting a call soon." Mr. Petrowski laughs and breaks the nervous tension of the room. Mitzie, the youngest granddaughter of the founder of Harper Marble, is the last of the girls to get married. Already in Mitzi's twenty-four years she had sued twelve times. Carl handled all of those cases.

As Mr. Petrowski continues to speak, Angela tunes him out, shocked that she has been given the Harper account to manage in Carl's absence. She feels honored that he would entrust her with the client, and smiles as she thinks her time behind the scenes on virtually every major case the firm has handled over the course of the past few years may be ending. His willingness to make her the lead contact person for a major client of the firm is a great sign she may have a future career here. She secretly plays out a number of scenarios in her head involving a devastated bride threatening to call her attorney.

To her delight, the call does not take as long as she thought it would. Less than two weeks after Mr. Petrowski's meeting, Angela has a message from Mitzie. Sandra, her secretary, takes the call. Sandra is a tall, thin, efficient lady in her early fifties. Though easy to work with, Sandra sometimes allows her personal life to take over. Constantly fighting with her boyfriends on the phone, Sandra has been known to break down crying in front of Angela more than once. Angela doesn't mind her outbursts, as long as she gets her work done. And she does. On some days, Angela actually welcomes the outbursts and crying. They remind her of humanity, something all together lacking on most days in the law firm. Mitzie, in tears on the telephone with Sandra, nervously schedules an appointment to meet with Angela the next day.

In the firm's conference room, Mitzie explains to Angela, "I had the dress all picked out, sized and on order. Mr. Frieston promised it would be ready on time, and I was paying him in installments. The dress was $20,000 and I only had $1,000 to go and the sneak puts it up for sale!" She grabs the tissue Angela is offering her and blows her nose rather loudly.

"So I called him up and asked him why he was going to sell it and he said Robert's mother had called and said I didn't want it . . . and that . . . that they had chosen another dress and tailor! So, he let some other girl buy it. It was mine!"

"So you're upset with the dressmaker?" Angela clarifies. Mitzie nods. "And you want your dress back?" Mitzie nods.

Angela sits for a moment thinking about her client's dilemma as Mitzie tries to dry her tears. Angela scoots her chair closer to Mitzie, puts her hand on her arm and says "Mitzie, You've got bigger problems than the dressmaker. Now I know you've come here for my legal advice, but I'm going to give you another piece of advice and you are welcome to take it or leave it."

"You had better think long and hard about marrying into a family with so little respect for a new bride's choice of wedding gowns. This woman who called your dressmaker and made other plans for you does not have your best interest in mind. She will be your mother-in-law, and I can't think of a worse position to be in no matter how much you love Robert. And, I'm willing to guess that Robert did not stand up for you, speak to his mother, or understand the problem. Am I right?"

"Well yeah . . . I guess I never thought about it that way either. I just thought it was wrong of the dressmaker to sell my dress," Mitzie says.

"Well, it was wrong of the dressmaker to sell your dress after you had paid so much on it. But, I think it was even more wrong of your future mother-in-law to interfere in that way. I'll try to get back your dress and/or your money, but I can't make any promises. Meanwhile, you really need to think this out, Mitzie, and direct fault where it's due."

"Thank you so much. And thank you for pointing that out to me. I feel so stupid for not having thought of it sooner. I guess I was so mad at the dressmaker I wasn't thinking right. I'll call you tomorrow." Mitzie hugs Angela and then leaves her alone with her notepad in the conference room. "That wasn't nearly as difficult as I thought it was going to be. . . . That poor girl," she thinks to herself.

Angela takes some time alone in the conference room to take notes on everything Mitzie reported. In the middle of her notes, Angela closes her eyes to relax, propping her head on her hand. Rather unexpectedly, she finds herself entering the front side door of a church. She turns to her left and takes a few steps forward, aware there are others behind her. The area surrounding her is dark, but she can see light pouring in at the other end of the church's foyer through another open door. She places her left hand directly out to her side and braces herself on the wall. The lower portion of the wall is covered in square panels of beautifully crafted wood. Her hand is in the center of one of these panels. Her eyes adjust and her surroundings become clear.

A heavenly glow emanates from above her head. She looks up toward the light source. Her heart skips a beat, her breath shallows, and she is awestruck by a beautiful vision of stained glass. Its tall, narrow, plain beauty calls to her, comforting and reassuring her. She bathes in its soft, glowing embrace. It is as if her soul becomes one with the light, sparkling through the stained glass like light waltzing though diamonds. Angela feels peace, warmth and security.

She looks down and notices she is dressed in white. There is also white material draped over her left arm, which remains on the wall. To her right is the center aisle of the church, leading to the congregation. She is not quite ready to step forward.

The vision ends just as quickly as it begins and Angela finds herself seated at the conference table of her firm once again. She is shaken by the unexpected vision but marvels at the beauty of the tall narrow stained glass window. It was not a typical stained glass window, as it had no religious symbols or biblical depictions. It was made up of small diamond cuts, with small engravings inside each triangle. The engravings looked like spades in an old deck of cards with panes of deep ocean blue appearing to flow down together with a glowing white light at Angela's feet.

Angela returns to her office. Sandra, noticing the blankness of Angela's stare and stiffness of stride, cautiously asks, "Did it go okay?"

"Yes. It did . . . Hold all my calls." Angela replies as she enters her office and closes the door behind her.

She sits in a guest chair in the corner of her office contemplating the vision she has just witnessed. She does not feel comfortable sitting behind her own desk yet. How could she be instantly transported to another place? What was this church? Where was this church and why was she there? Suddenly, Angela feels taller. She feels like the lady she saw in the mirror on the train. This may have been her wedding, but she didn't see her husband. This church must be connected to the newlywed couple on the train and the honeymoon, she thinks to herself, rubbing her temples with her hands. Angela feels like it is her church, that she belongs there, in this very important occasion. She is left only to conclude it is her wedding, based on the honeymoon dreams and white draping material. And, incredibly contrary to Angela in every way, she feels proud to be Catholic.

Angela's sanity breaks as a mix of confusion and doubts rushes through her mind. Nothing makes sense anymore and she is convinced she is suddenly living a dual life. She's taking over someone else's body, with someone else's emotions, dreams, fear, love, and now, religion. The religion part is the most problematic, as Angela doesn't want to think about any of it. Feeling a reverence toward a faith she has never in her life been a part of is, in light of her past experience with religion, more than she thinks she can handle. Her mind switches between sanity and nonsensical rambling as she draws up her knees to hug them tight in the chair, trying desperately to stop thinking, to stop feeling like this other woman.

Overruled

It happened shortly after Angela turned thirteen and lasted until the end of her eighth grade year in 1985. She loved to read books and had already finished reading the classics in the school's limited library twice— classics such as *The Adventures of Huckleberry Finn, Tom Sawyer, Animal Farm* and others. She devoured books and relished in their generous gifts of alternative realities.

Her friends also discovered the gift of books early on and routinely traded them amongst themselves. Of course, religious stories and inspirational testimonials made up the bulk of the books traded. The parents were buying them after all. But Angela, already bored with the religious books, had discovered the spellbinding works of Stephen King and V. C. Andrews, best selling authors during that time.

One winter evening on a December day in 1984, Angela and her best friend Mandy Wilson traded books. Mandy, a bright, cheerful girl Angela's age, had a gift for music and comedy. She always made her friends laugh and her magnetic personality attracted Angela to her the first day she attended the Christian school, just two years before. Angela and Mandy quickly became inseparable best friends, sharing everything and helping one another become teenagers in the strict and legalistic framework they called life. They both had come to expect the ridiculous with regards to rules and regulations, but they could never prepare themselves for what came next, or how it would change their lives forever.

Mandy, also an avid reader, had begun anxiously reading Angela's copy of *Pet Sematary* by Stephen King. The book had been a quick and enjoyable read for Angela, who couldn't help but eagerly recommend it to Mandy. Worried the cover of the book, a crazed resurrected cat, might trigger concerns from her zealous fundamental Baptist parents, Mandy wisely hides the book in her bedroom and reads it after bedtime under covers with a small flashlight.

She takes it to school where she'll have more time to read. She decides she will read it in homeroom and during class breaks after she completes her assigned work. One Friday morning, she places it on top of her desk with her school books before homeroom. Just before the school bell rings, she goes into the hallway to drink from the water fountain. When Mandy returns, her homeroom teacher, Mrs. Brooks, is thumbing through the book and defiantly refuses to return it. Unable to contact Angela or speak to her teacher or parent about the book, Mandy spends the entire weekend nervously pacing around her home and biting her long fingernails.

The next Monday morning, Mandy runs nervously over to Angela, who is placing her books into her locker in the back of their classroom. Finally she can talk to her best friend, who had been on a weekend trip with relatives. "Ang . We need to talk. I think we're in big trouble".

"What did we do now?" Angela asks, slamming

her locker shut and balancing a stack of books in her arms.

"Friday, when you were out," Mandy whispers, "Mrs. Brooks took your book off my desk and started reading it. I asked her to give it back and she wouldn't. I think she took it to the school board!"

"Which book? The one I gave you last week? *Pet Sematary?*" Angela asks.

"Yeah."

"What did she say?"

"Just that she didn't think I should be reading it," explains Mandy. "I think she saw a cuss word."

"That's ridiculous!" Angela says in a loud whisper, rolling her eyes. "Lots of books in the library have cuss words in them. It's not like we've never heard them before. And if she takes it to the school board, that means the church board saw it too. They're the same you know?"

A loud ringing sound interrupts their conversation and calls for everyone's attention as the students pause to look at the speaker, a circular disk filled with holes over the chalkboard.

"Mandy Harper, Please report to the principal's office," the office secretary announces to the entire school. Everyone turns to look at Mandy, whose brown curls seem less bouncy than usual while her large green eyes appear frozen in terror. She looks at Angela and says simply, "It's okay. It's only a book."

Mandy reluctantly puts her books on her desk, hugs Angela with a nervous look, and walks out of the classroom to start downstairs toward the office. Angela, confused and trying to think why the book would be so terrible for them to read, takes her seat. The teacher, Mrs. Brooks, rises from her desk in the front left corner of the room and begins taking attendance.

Angela tries desperately to concentrate on her schoolwork but can't stop thinking about Mandy. Surely this is no big deal, she thinks to herself. Surely Mandy will just be scolded and have to write some bible verses one hundred times for punishment. Finally, after almost an hour passes on the clock next to the chalkboard, Mandy slowly opens the classroom's door. She goes over to her desk next to Angela's and retrieves her books. Angela can see the pain in her eyes and the tear stained tissue hidden in her right hand. Her broken voice whispers "Two weeks," to Angela as she gathers her things. But Angela hears so much more.

Angela immediately understands her best friend has been suspended and her worst fears have come true; she was paddled, and would surely receive another as soon as she gets home. It wasn't the first time she saw a friend of hers after they had been paddled. They all had the same broken and defeated look. No matter what her friends' temperaments were, the paddlings always reached more than skin deep. With each strike, something untouchable left the child. Respect was the first thing to go, for themselves and then for the person inflicting the blows. Second was self confidence, especially when the paddling was for something small or an unanticipated infraction. Last to go was trust. It was never about the pain. It was supposed to be about love.

The paddling room is the far stairwell at the end of the school's hall. Framed with cement walls painted light green, it has a black metal staircase perfect for holding up small children's weight as they bend over. Large heavy metal doors close tight from the hallway to muffle the children's screams. On the wall, protruding from the cement are nails holding wooden paddles with thin leather straps. Each paddle is one foot long and two inches thick. The most painful ones have holes in them. Sometimes Angela is there because she talks during class, other times it's because she speaks her mind. She's always getting in trouble for that. Three licks are the norm.

But perhaps even worse than the spankings, as far as Angela is concerned, for at thirteen she now well endures their painful sting, is the prayer that follows. "In love" they say to the children as they force them to their knees to pray, "Spare the rod and spoil the child."

Was God really responsible for this? Did he really want them to hurt her and her friends this way? It was times like these that Angela began to dislike their god. If she were to some day have the power to create her own version of God, He would never hurt her or her friends this way.

Angela worries about Mandy as she walks out of their classroom. Her parents are on their way to the school. Angela knows they will blame her for the trouble their daughter is in. How could she do this to her best friend? But how was she supposed to know? She never brought her Stephen King book to school but never stopped to think what could happen if she did. Apparently, Mandy hadn't either.

Angela, opening her math book and trying to turn her attention back to the teacher, the chalkboard, and the day's math lesson, is surprised to hear yet another announcement over the loud speaker. This time, it's for her.

"Angela Grubbs, please report to the principal's office." She looks around at her friends, who silently stare back at her with looks of support, as she stands and is excused from the classroom.

Angela's mind goes blank, unable to comprehend the gravity of her situation or the reality of the moment.

She figures they've seen her name inside the front cover of the book and are calling her to retrieve it. She reports to the principal's office, which is on the floor directly under her classroom. She walks pass the secretary and into the large spacious office she has only seen once before when retrieving a book for a teacher several years ago. The principal, Mr. Sands, is seated behind a desk facing the door. His tall square figure matches his tall green leather square armchair. His neck is invisible under his dress shirt and necktie. His knobby hands ring together with excitement as a fake smile spreads across his face.

As Angela enters, she notices there are three chairs in front of his clean desk. In the center of the desk is her book, with numerous small white pieces of papers marking portions of the text. On one side of his desk is a large brand new black bible. He asks Angela to close the door and motions for her to sit down in one of the chairs.

She takes her seat, crosses her legs under her long skirt and folds her hands in her lap, the way she has been taught all girls should sit. Mr. Sands places his right hand on the book and asks slowly, "Angela, is this your book?"

Without hesitation, Angela responds, "Yes sir. I even put my name in the front of it."

"Have you read it?"

"Yes, sir, I have."

"Did you like it?"

"Yes, sir. Stephen King is one of my favorite authors." Angela answers honestly.

Mr. Sands shakes his head, closes his eyes and lifts the book from the desk. "We are so disappointed in you Angela," he says as he thumbs through the pages of the paperback book. "Did you know this book is full of curse words?"

"Yes sir. Lots of books have cuss words," she says in the book's defense. "Some of the books in our own library have them, and they're required reading for English classes." She reminds him.

Mr. Sands pauses, ignores her comments and opens the *Pet Sematary* paperback book to a pre-marked page. "This however, is unacceptable." He says, looking down on the page and back up at Angela. "THIS book has sex in it!"

Angela, astonished at his outburst, sits a moment in silence trying to consider his point of view. Everything suddenly becomes clear. They are going to pin this on her. They don't like her so they are going to use this little book to get rid of her. Many kids have gone before her, but she's never been in this degree of trouble before. They hated the other kids, many of them her friends, and disgraced their names in church, but she always believed she was somehow safe from all of that. Her mind races. Her knees begin to shake. Somehow, she is a threat to them. It's as if the entire school and church board routinely gangs up on the children, constantly trying to catch them doing something wrong. Angela suspects this is somehow connected to their own delusions of grandeur. By punishing children they somehow feel better about themselves. But sex was not a topic she envisioned speaking to her principal about. She wouldn't have brought the book to school because of the graphic image of a scary resurrected cat on the cover of the book. It looked demonic, and anything remotely demonic was not allowed. That she understood. But sex? It wasn't even remotely on her mind.

She suddenly feels no respect for the sick, shriveled up ego she sees sitting behind the other side of the desk. She now understands his agenda and knows he is going to attack her. "You found the two-paragraph sex scene?" she says calmly, feeling a powerful strength rising within her. "You and the entire church board read the book over the weekend in order to find that little scene, didn't you?" She asks, a small grin tracing across her face.

"Well yes, we did read the book," he answers simply.

Angela takes another breath. "Then you also noticed that sex scene was only implied and it was between two married consenting adults?"

Mr. Sands pauses, not expecting such a response from Angela, much less a defense. He doesn't like her condescending tone. He won't tolerate it, he silently tells himself. "It is still filth. And a young impressionable mind such as yours should not be reading it!" he says as he slams the paperback book onto the desk.

"Song of Solomon is worse than anything you read in those paragraphs," says Angela, pointing to the book. "Surely the church board remembers their bible verses?"

"Don't talk back to me young lady. You're in big trouble. You are going to be suspended today for distributing filthy literature!" he says, waving his finger at Angela.

"What? I've never heard of any rule like that! That's a rule you just made up to suspend me isn't it?" she demands, well aware of the strict rules which have confined her all her life.

"No. The entire board backs this decision. You will be suspended for one week. Mandy was suspended for two weeks. During that time you will not be allowed to do school work, but you will be allowed to make it all up when you return from your suspension. Your parents have been notified and they should arrive shortly."

"This is unbelievable," says Angela. "You're really serious aren't you?"

"Yes, I am serious. And that's not all. The board has met and it is our decision that you should not continue at this school next year. We will make an exception and allow you to finish the school year, but you will not be welcome back for your ninth grade year."

"Did you expel Mandy too?" asks Angela, still shocked.

"No. Her situation is different. She is welcome to stay. We feel that you have become a bad apple and, one bad apple can infect the entire bunch," he says, staring flatly at Angela.

All bets are off. Angela has lost. She knows that anyone expelled from the school is also expelled from the church. They are taking away everything she has ever known without any warning at all. There will be no redemption. There has been no sin. Her confidence turns to rage mixed with rejection and uncertainty. Angela quietly stands and reaches for her book.

Mr. Sands takes the book away before she can touch it. "No. That stays here until I speak with your parents."

She begins to walk out of the office, his words *"bad apple . . . bad apple . . ."* repeating over and over in her head. As she reaches for the door, something makes her stop. She spins back around to face his desk one last time. She places both of her hands on the desk and leans forward so she is within inches of Mr. Sand's face. Mr. Sands, obviously uncomfortable, says nothing as he backs away from Angela.

Angela's voice lowers and her eyes flatten. Knowing she has nothing left to lose, she is free to speak her mind. She looks Mr. Sands straight in the eyes and begins. "Let me tell you something, Mr. Sands. I've been a member of this school and church since I was three years old. I am now thirteen. You've only been here two years and I bet I've have seen and heard hypocrisy that you could only dream of in your worse nightmares. And now you want to call me a bad apple? Well, I am *exactly* what this school made me!" She says as she slams her open hand on his desk next to the Stephen King book. Mr. Sands, slightly dazed, says nothing as Angela slowly turns and leaves his office, silently daring him to say one more word to her.

She returns to her classroom, gathers her books and puts on her large black wool coat and hat. Without speaking to anyone, she walks out of the school building to wait outside for her parents. She places her books on a small concrete wall next to the parking lot, jumps up to sit next to them and begins wondering why sex is such an evil thing. For the first time she doesn't worry about the concrete running or picking her pantyhose. She would just as soon tear them into shreds with her bare hands, strip naked and walk through the school halls proudly demonstrating her God-given body. A small grin spreads across her face as she imagines the scene: Little old teachers shrieking in horror, scrambling to cover bulging eyes as the boys cheer her on. The men would all be chasing her, eager to tackle her nude body and cover it up, all pretending to be concerned, but quietly excited.

Her parent's arrival halts her rebellious daydream and forces her to face reality yet again. They greet her cautiously, not knowing why they have both been called to the school.

"Angela. What's going on?" Luther asks.

"You're not going to believe it. They're kicking me

out of school for letting Mandy borrow my Stephen King book."

"Kicking you out?!" Brenda cries, "but why?"

Angela can only say, "you'll have to ask them."

Luther passes Angela a set of keys and tells her to wait for them in their car, still warm from the drive over. Angela hops down from the wall, gathers her things from the concrete wall and calmly strolls to the car to wait as she is told. When she arrives at the car, she fumbles the keys in the lock as newly arrived tears begin to block her vision. In the car, she lays her head on the back of the seat and tries to sort out her feelings. Part of her knows it is finally time to move on. Another part of her suspects things will never again be the same. Tears stream down her emotionless face. They come from her tired and religiously spent young soul.

Brenda and Luther are not made to wait. Mr. Sands is waiting for them in his office as they arrive. The book is still dramatically centered on his desk. They all greet each other and take their seats. Mr. Sands begins.

"We found this book on the desk of your daughter's best friend. Your daughter signed her name in the front and has admitted to me that it is her book. We thought you would like to know," he says, his voice reflecting both pride and concern. He is sure her parents will be pleased with the school's vigilance for their child's salvation.

"What part did you feel we should know?" Luther asks seriously as he crosses his legs and folds his hands together.

"Well," stumbles Mr. Sands, "that your daughter was reading this filth and let her classmates read it."

"Mr. Sands," says Luther, "we bought that book for Angela. We let her read it."

"Oh. Well perhaps you didn't know that it has curse words and a sex scene in it? I've marked the pages for you to review," he says as he pushes the book forward towards Luther. Brenda remains speechless, happily allowing her husband to address this strange situation.

"That won't be necessary," Luther says, motioning him to stop with his right hand in the air. "So, are you trying to tell me that my daughter is in trouble for owning this book?" He asks as he lowers his voice and lifts one eyebrow.

"Well. Uh, no sir. She's in trouble for distributing filthy literature in the school."

Luther beings to chuckle and Mr. Sands struggles to continue. This is not going as well as he hoped. He thought these parents would be as easy to convince as Mandy's parents. They are apparently not as godly as he thought. "You see," he explains. "We have an unwritten policy here, Mr. Grubbs, that school age children, especially girls, should not be reading such secular filth and bringing it to school to hand out to others."

Brenda interrupts. "Mandy brought the book to school, not Angela."

"But Angela gave the book to Mandy."

"Yes," admits Luther, "but that happened at our house, not school. Our daughter did not bring the book to school."

"Well," Mr. Sands shifts in his seat and straightens his back "the church board has reviewed the book and voted unanimously to suspend Mandy and Angela. Angela will have a one-week suspension, Mandy will have two. The board has also determined that Angela will not be welcomed back here for her ninth grade year, but we are generously allowing her to complete this year since it's almost over."

Brenda and Luther, luckily already prepared for this news by Angela, do not flinch. But, in order to clarify, Luther asks, "So you are expelling Angela for simply owning a book you don't approve of?"

"It's not just that Mr. Grubbs. We know your wife and daughter have attended our church for many years, but we rarely see you. I believe it is having a negative influence on your daughter and her outspoken strong opinions are infecting the other children. She is a leader and corrupting influence on others. This book is really all the proof we need. And now you admit you let her read this filth at such a tender age."

"Mr. Sands, my wife and I allow our daughter to read this because at the tender age of thirteen she is very mature and reading on a college level. She's already read all the books in your library and the *Nancy Drew* series, which I'm sure you wouldn't approve of either. I'm proud to buy her whatever books on the bestseller list I feel she can handle and I will continue to do so despite your ignorant advice."

"And," says Brenda, "I agree with your decision to expel her at the end of the year. I believe she has gotten a great education here, but I don't see your high school curriculum offering her much."

"Oh, you are mistaken, Mrs. Grubbs. Our high school curriculum is one of the best and cutting edge of any Christian school you'll find in Georgia."

"Really?" asks Luther, "then where are all the computers? Why aren't you teaching programming? And my daughter will go to college when she graduates, and I'm pretty sure she is not going to choose Bob Jones University now."

Mr. Sands stands. "Well then I believe we've said all that's necessary." He graciously offers his hand for a shake. Luther ignores his outstretched hand. "Thank you for such an informative meeting, Mr. Sands," he says as he takes the book from Mr. Sand's desk and leaves the office with hand around Brenda's waist.

Angela completes the suspension and returns to school only to find she's expected to make up all of her quizzes and tests. "No problem," she thinks confidently. She spent most of her days in suspension reading and studying from her textbooks and feels prepared. But bible class is different. Bible class is always different.

Mrs. Brooks, their regular bible teacher is absent when Angela returns. She's busy giving birth to her seventh child, dutifully being fruitful and multiplying. In her place, the children have the distinct honor of having the church's first lady, Mrs. Loman, the preacher's wife. She's a small, mousy lady. Everything about her is flat except her hair, which curves and feathers, plastered in place with *Aquanet* hairspray, a small can of which can always be found in her purse.

Mrs. Loman takes Angela outside the classroom, seats her in the hallway and gives her two complete chapter citations from the King James Version of the bible. She expects Angela to write coma for coma, colon for colon, period for period, the entire bible verses from memory.

Angela is accustomed to these kinds of tests. She has been making good scores on them since elementary school as her memory is excellent. But every year they grow longer, more complicated and require more study. And this time Angela cannot complete the quizzes because she was never warned which verses would be tested for memorization. She has no choice but to turn them in blank.

Mrs. Loman takes the papers, looks down at their blankness and glares at Angela, who returns frustrated to her assigned seat. Mrs. Loman bends over her newly acquired desk in the front left corner of the classroom, writes something down, grabs a stack of already graded papers and begins handing them to the students.

She hands out everyone's results and comes over to Angela's desk last. She looks down at her and begins placing the empty pages with a large, bright red "F" in front of Angela one by one.

"Angela. You failed this one." She says as the paper hits hard in front of her on the desk. "And, you failed this one . . . and this one . . . and this one. What kind of a Christian woman do you think you'll be when you grow up?" she shouts.

Angela, shocked, begins to feel a faint boiling sensation running though her veins. She knows better than to say anything and can only stare back at this crazed woman hoping her eyes will warn her to stop. She's never felt so angry before. Mrs. Loman nonetheless continues.

"You must not think the bible is important now that you've found more interesting things to read. Lots of people who didn't think the bible was important are burning in hell." She says with an evil, hateful tone Angela and her friends have never heard from her before.

Angela's head becomes light, the room dims, her mouth feels heavy and her palms begin to sweat. She knows if she opens her mouth it will all be over. She is certain her tongue is capable of shredding stupid little Mrs. Loman into a million pieces. She wants to kick her ass.

Mrs. Loman strides confidently back to the front of the classroom to stand behind the wooden podium. The rest of the children in the classroom are silent, shocked to have witnessed an apparently mean side to what they thought was a godly woman. They secretly exchange incredulous looks while Mrs. Loman peers down over her lesson plans, propped up on the podium.

Angela sensors herself and remains quiet, reacting only with her body, which she positions away from Mrs. Loman. She has to completely turn around in her seat to stare at the girl behind her, Samantha. Samantha, one of her best friends since second grade, can see that Angela, normally a well-behaved and level-headed friend, is about to lose her temper. She whispers to Angela, "It's okay. Calm down, it will be over soon." The children are all partners in this place, helping one another to make it through.

"Turn around, Angela Grubbs." Mrs. Loman demands more than once. Defiantly, Angela turns her head from Samantha to the front of the class, cuts her eyes at Mrs. Loman and returns to stare at Samantha seated behind her. Samantha looks around nervously, feeling the tension thicken the air in the room, making it harder for everyone to breathe.

Mrs. Loman decides to continue her attack on Angela in a more generalized way, making the lesson for the day: The importance of reading your bible. She begins. "Now we all know that there are many choices for us when it comes to books. We should choose wisely when deciding what to read. God has given us a wonderful book that we should all read daily. If you've read it once through cover to cover already, maybe you should do it again. If you think you already know everything in the book. Think again. You'll always find something new. It's not like any book you'd read out of a bookstore . . .

"As Christian youth, you should all be taking great care to read things appropriate for you." She stops and looks over at Angela, still sitting with her back to her with eyes closed. Her words have hit Angela one after another like poison daggers in her back. Mrs. Loman continues her sermon, making many references to secular versus biblical readings. Heaven will reward faithful readers while hell will destroy and burn others . . ." It's not long before her words reach the end of Angela's rope.

Twenty years later, Angela will not be able to recall which poison dagger caused her to finally fight back. She grabs her bible off of her desktop and throws it across the room at Mrs. Loman. Before Samantha or her other friends can catch her, Angela swings around and out of her chair, lunges forward and yells, "YOU WILL NOT TALK ABOUT ME THAT WAY! YOU FUCKING BITCH! I WILL SEE YOU IN HELL!!!"

Mrs. Loman drops everything, moves to her right to dodge the bible as it flails through the air toward her. She races from the podium to behind her desk, sure Angela is about to throw more things or hit her as she advances toward her, face reddened and eyes filled with what she is sure is Satan himself.

Angela, blind with rage and shaking, feels the hands of her childhood friends reach out to restrain her. Luckily, through her blinding rage, Angela sees the terror in Mrs. Loman's eyes. Angela gives an evil smile, sure Mrs. Loman has soiled her underwear.

Angela runs out of the classroom door, down the stairs and to the front office to use the phone. "I need to use the phone," she advises the school secretary, who, after taking one glance at Angela's demeanor, does not hesitate to lift the phone onto the counter. Angela calls her mother to tell her she needs to leave work and pick her up from school right away. Although she doesn't explain anything right away, she promises to as soon as she arrives. Her mother trusts her, and arrives shortly after Angela hangs up the phone and rushes out of the school building to wait on the church steps.

"I don't know what happened," she tells her parents later that evening. "I just lost control. I have never been so mad at anyone in my life. I know I shouldn't have done it, but I couldn't help it."

Brenda and Luther stare at her across the dinner table in absolute shock. They speak in private many times about Angela. They have seen a change in her that they aren't sure how to handle. They blame it on puberty, that pre-teen angst they are constantly warned about. Angela is sometimes dramatic, like most pre-teen girls, but this was exceptional.

Luther silently eats his dinner, allowing Angela to describe everything that happened to her today. Angela nervously recounts the events, sure that her failing grades and violent behavior will result in restriction. She finishes her story, careful to tell it just as it happened since she's already in so much trouble.

To her shock, her parents don't act surprised or put her on restriction. She's not sure what is going on in their heads. Her father says nothing other than, "We'll take you to school in the morning. We will need to speak with the principal again." He looks across the table at Brenda, who nods in agreement.

Angela goes to bed sick at her stomach. She is sure

her world is ending and she fears her parent's retribution more than the school or church's board. She knows they will not tolerate her attack on the preacher's wife. She knows she will be punished severely.

The next school day is dreary and cold, as she climbs into the back of the family car. Luther has already drunk three cups of coffee and her mother sits silently staring out the car window. They have hardly spoken a word to Angela, who isolated herself in her room after dinner the night before. Shortly before 11pm, she heard her parents whispering through the thin walls that separated her room from theirs. She was sure they were talking about her and what kind of punishment she deserved, but she couldn't make out a sound.

Their car turns into the parking lot onto the wet pavement. School buses and vans line up to drop children out onto the sidewalk leading to the school's building, tucked behind the church's chapel. The school bell announcing the beginning of classes will soon ring. Angela's parents separate from her as she reluctantly heads to her homeroom. Her parents go in the other direction, to speak to the principal. To Angela's surprise, the school principal did not call her home the night before. Angela thinks nothing has been said about her outburst yesterday. But she couldn't be more wrong. Nobody called her home because they were busy at church.

Last night marked the one-year anniversary of the church's women's bible group. A group of sixty church women met every Monday night for bible study. Topics of discussion ranged from who had the best tuna casserole recipe to how to properly submit to their husband's dominating role in the family. Angela's mother was not a member, but over half of the mothers of her classmates were. The topic that night centered around unruly children, and the story of Angela's sudden demonic possession ruled the evening's conversations.

"You could see the devil in that child's eye," Mrs. Loman says, as others listen to her story, spellbound.

"Well, you can't let her continue at the school," another mother protests.

"Absolutely not. Who knows what she's capable of doing?" another sounds from the back of the room.

They are quick to condemn Angela, even though they all know her to be a good girl. She's a member of the church choir, a cheerleader at school and on the honor roll. They see her prior reputation as an indication of how fast and far Satan can pull you down rather than a testimony to Angela's true character.

Finally, the mothers come to the only conclusion that they can: to prohibit their children from having any contact with Angela Grubbs. Mrs. Loman promises something will be done about Angela's behavior, and assures them their children are in no danger. At next week's meeting, Mrs. Loman will share with everyone what punishment and what recourses are available to them, for their own children's salvation is always at risk.

A week later, after all is said and done, Angela will be pulled aside during gym class and told not to speak to or play with others. If she does, they will get into trouble, as her teacher has strict instructions from the parents to report any contact their children have with Angela Grubbs. Angela will be forced to complete the last twelve weeks of school in a virtual silent hell. She'll be crushed as they will successfully exclude her from her entire world, childhood and friends.

Angela takes her assigned seat in her homeroom class, secretly wishing Mandy was back at school from her suspension so she could talk to her. She needed her friend. She wanted desperately to see if she was doing okay, to see if she held any ill will toward her. But she knew under the circumstances that that was impossible. She tried to call, but Mandy's mother slammed down the phone after yelling, "NEVER CALL HERE AGAIN!"

Meanwhile, downstairs in Mr. Sands' office, Luther and Brenda are furious. "How could you allow any teacher to verbally degrade and belittle a child in your school? That is unacceptable!" Luther says firmly.

"I assure you, Mr. Grubbs, nobody degraded or belittled Angela. Our teachers would not do anything like that."

"So are you calling my daughter and I liars?"

"No sir! I'm sure this is just some sort of misunderstanding."

"What is there not to understand? My daughter would never act out in such a way unless she was provoked. She has never ever had any problems with anger or violence in her entire time at this school. You have her school record, look in it. And, if this school has taught her anything, it's not to lie!"

"That won't be necessary. I know your child well. I'm just saying maybe she didn't communicate properly what really happened."

"Well why don't we invite her down so she can communicate it to you? We told you exactly what she told us. Why would she lie about behaving like she did?"

The intercom in Angela's classroom buzzes loudly and announces Angela was needed in the principal's office. This time, it isn't unexpected. Angela, tired and withdrawn from the others, stands up and walks out of the door without so much as a glance towards Mrs.

Loman, who is seated once again behind Mrs. Brooks' desk.

Once in Mr. Sands' office, she takes a seat next to her parents. Her father is sitting in front of Mr. Sands' desk with his arms folded and an angry look on his face. Angela is sure he is angry at her. Her mother also looks serious and is sitting rigidly in her chair with her legs crossed and hands firmly gripping the arm rails to her chair.

"Angela. I want you to tell Mr. Sands exactly what happened yesterday." Luther says calmly to Angela, who nervously looks back at her father.

"Yes, sir," she says as she sits forward to face Mr. Sands. "Well, yesterday was my first day back from suspension. When we got to bible class, Mrs. Loman pulled me out of the classroom and gave me some bible verses to write down from memorization. I was never given the list of verses to memorize while I was out, so I wasn't prepared and I failed them all.

"Then, she started passing out grades and came to me last. She said 'Angela, you failed this one, and that one' and then she asked me what kind of Christian woman I was going to be and reminded me that people who don't think the bible is important burn in hell. I got really mad about it and turned around in my seat, but didn't say anything. She started bible class and kept talking about reading good books like the bible and not secular books. She kept on and wouldn't stop." Luther quietly cheers as his daughter recounts the same damning testimonial she recounted to him and his wife the night before.

"Finally, I lost my temper." Angela says nervously, looking away from Mr. Sands momentarily. "I got up, threw the bible at her, called her a . . . bitch . . . and told her I'd see her in hell." Mr. Sands stares at Angela, shocked at what he has just heard. "Angela," he advises, "you must have taken something out of context. Mrs. Loman is a wonderful Christian woman. She's the preacher's wife. I'm sure she can clear this whole thing up. Let's call her in here." He rises from his chair, goes into the hall and calls Mrs. Loman to his office from the speaker behind the secretary's desk. Angela glances nervously over at her parents and slightly grins when her father confidently gives her a wink of an eye. They add another chair and arrange the seats in two rows of two in front of the principal's desk.

Mrs. Loman confidently enters the office with Mr. Sands and takes the chair next to Angela, in front of her parents. He clears his throat and begins.

"Mrs. Loman. Apparently, something happened yesterday during your eighth grade bible class, in which Ms. Grubbs is a student. Can you tell us what happened?" asks Mr. Sands.

"Well," she begins slowly in a quiet sweet voice, "Angela was out all last week so there were several bible verses she needed to make up. I put her out in the hall to take the quizzes and she failed every one."

Luther interrupts, "Did you give her the assigned verses to work on while she was suspended?"

"Well no," Mrs. Loman explains, "Her regular teacher, Mrs. Brooks, was here all last week before she went into labor. I assumed she gave Angela the assignments."

"No, mam. I didn't receive any assignments for bible class." Angela calmly states.

"Well," Mrs. Loman continues, "she did very poorly on the quizzes. After she finished, I called roll and then passed out the grades to everyone. Then, we had class as usual. Nothing odd really." She says calmly, looking over at Angela, unaware Angela has already told her side of the story.

Angela's mouth hangs open involuntarily, as she gasps and stares at Mrs. Loman in disbelief. She cannot overcome the fact that the preacher's wife is telling a bold faced lie to her, her parents and the principal. For the first time in her life, an adult has lied to her face in order to save her skin and hang poor little Angela out to dry. Angela will take no part in it.

"That's not true and you know it." She says sharply as Mr. Sands tries to interrupt her. "There are thirty other students upstairs that will tell you the real story. I can't believe that you would sit here and lie like that, preacher's wife and all! How dare you?"

"Angela!" Mr. Sands cries disapprovingly. Mrs. Loman stares at her with a slight grin, hoping her temper will flare again to her benefit. But it doesn't. Instead, Angela looks her level in the eyes and without moving an inch, lowers her voice and says, "I was willing to own up to my bad behavior. If you had any decency in you, you would too."

Angela's father stands and takes his jacket from the back of his chair. "I think we've heard all we need to hear today. It's obvious Mrs. Loman is lying and frankly, I'm shocked given your position in the church. And, Mr. Sands, you don't have to worry about Angela returning to this school next year, like we discussed earlier, there is certainly nothing more you can offer her here."

Confused, Angela follows her parents out of the office and into the hallway. "What just happened in there? Am I not in trouble?" Angela asks, wondering why she hasn't been suspended again or had any new punishment inflicted upon her.

Angela's mother places her arm around her and whispers, "That my dear, was a lesson in truth. We are proud of you for standing up to them. I know it wasn't easy. And, I promise you won't have to come back to this school next year. You've learned an important lesson today. Sometimes people lie, but if you are always honest to yourself, you can't go wrong."

Luther hugs Angela tight, kisses her on the cheek and says, "Thanks for not making me look like an idiot. I told them you would tell the truth, and you did. Mrs. Loman was wrong and we know you'd never act that way unless you were really provoked."

Third Party Advice

Angela sits alone in purgatory. That's how she views hospital waiting rooms: purgatories filled with poor souls desperately waiting to hear the fate of their loved ones. She's waiting for her father, Luther, to bring hot chocolate from the vending machine down the hall. "This is it Dad. The last time we'll wait in waiting rooms for Mom to get out of eye surgery." The doctors had told Brenda that they wouldn't be able to do any more surgeries on her, not even experimental.

"Well, she'll be ok, Luther replies, "She has to. She bounced back pretty well last year after she hurt her back. We'll just wait here until we have word. Did you get all her things on your way in from your office? You know she loves her poofy bedroom shoes," he says, ringing his hands in his lap as he bends forward to stare at the floor. He hates hospitals and can't wait until she is free to go home. He also resents his new work, running specialized adventure tours for a travel agency. His work will take him away from home the entire next month. So, Brenda must go home with Angela and Brent. "It's better that way," Luther silently reminds himself, as he knows Angela has taken care of her mother's eyes countless times and already knows the routine. Brenda won't have to stay with them long.

He'll pick her up and take her home as soon as he gets back from Australia.

"I've already taken everything to my house." Angela says, blowing the steam off her hot chocolate. "Brent fixed up the spare bedroom for her again."

"She spends so much time with you two. I don't know what I'd do without you. You're always taking such good care of her. You've always been like a little nurse, even when you were little. You'd run around taking care of your Granny, who was never well, God rest her soul."

Finally, a nurse announces Brenda is out of recovery and has been moved to a private room on the seventh floor. Angela and Luther make their way to the elevators, exhausted and wrought with anticipation to see her.

When they arrive at the room, Brenda is lying on her back motionless with both eyes covered with white patches, tape and metal disks. Angela is not surprised or moved by her mother's appearance. She has seen her mother like this on eight different occasions over the past ten years. She knows what her eyes look like under the patches, how many eye drops she'll require, which medicines she will need and how often they will be applied around the clock. She knows that the small box on the counter in the corner of the hospital room is filled with supplies for her to take home—eye patches, tape, sterile cotton balls, distilled water, and extra metal disks for protection. Angela knows the routine but doesn't welcome it.

"Angela?" Brenda whispers, her head turning slightly towards the door.

"Yes, Mom. It's me," she says taking her hand. "Dad and I are here. The doctor said you did great and should be able to see a little bit after all of this."

"I know, I talked to him. I've been up here for hours. What time is it? It was dark when I woke up."

Angela and Luther begin to laugh.

"Mom . . . I don't know how to tell you this but both of your eyes are covered and you are blind right now. It's going to be dark for a couple of days," she says patting her hand.

A smile streaks across Brenda's face as she begins to laugh. "I guess you're right! No wonder it's dark. I swear I was just layin' here trying to figure it out. I knew it was dark when we got here this mornin', I just couldn't believe the surgery took that long and you had left me here alone during the night. You always spend the night."

"How long have you been up here waiting?" asks Luther, pulling a chair close to her bedside and rubbing her hand.

"Too long. I'm so bored. I can listen to T.V, but I can't see a thing. Angela, will you tell me a story?"

"A story? I didn't bring any magazines up from the waiting room, but I can go get some."

"No. One of your stories . . . Have you had any more dreams of your lover?"

"Your lover?" Luther asks.

"Mom! I can't believe you! Yes Dad, I've been having some dreams that involve me being married to another man. Kind of like having an affair in my sleep. Mom loves to hear about them."

"Oh. Well, that's pretty strange."

"Tell me about it," her mother urges, "so what happened Angela? You've seen him again?"

Angela sits down on the side of her bed opposite of her father and begins relaying the story as her mother smiles and hangs on every word.

"He bought me a house. . . . He was so excited to show it to me. He had purchased it without me seeing it beforehand. We'd been married for a little while at this time. It wasn't before we were married. The dream started in the kitchen of the house. Whoever lived there before had just moved out and left some things on the kitchen counter to my left and a bucket on the kitchen floor. I was walking through the kitchen and he was behind me. I was looking at the kitchen walls, commenting on what a horrible color they had been painted. It was really ridiculous, like a bright orange or something. I specifically heard myself say 'Who paints a kitchen this color?'

"My husband is behind me the entire time, laughing and joking with me. Basically, making fun of me. 'We can paint it again. It's not going to be a problem' he says to me as we start to go out of the kitchen. I then step over something in the floor and there's a little tiny room or closet area that's opened up . . . I've never seen this in a house before . . . it looks like a pantry in between the kitchen and dining room. Anyway, it's painted a horrible color too! And, it's not even the same horrible color the kitchen is painted in. So, of course I have a comment for that too.

"Then, we step into the dining room. It's so beautiful. There's light pouring through the windows. I'm at the front of the house and if I turn to my left I can see all the way past the front door and staircase into a living room. It's so open and big. There's no furniture, but the hardwood floors shine and there's beautiful wood molding framing the entrances to the rooms. They're not doors, but large open entryways.

"Next, we go to the staircase and I'm loving all the wood details. I make a comment that this really feels like home and compliment my husband on his good taste. He laughs and tells me he wants to show me the upstairs now. So, I feel his hand touch the small of my back as we start up the stairs. I look down and notice that at the base of the stairs the banister curves slightly outward and I think that's a nice expensive detail. I feel my hands reach down to pick up my dress. It's a soft cotton material and the dress is long and flowing, but straight. That is my first clue that I've traveled in time again."

Luther interrupts, "Whoa! Traveled in time? I thought these were just dreams?"

"Oh hush!" Brenda swats in the air towards Luther's voice. "Be quiet and let her finish!"

"So, we start up the stairs and suddenly two children come running down the stairs almost knocking us down. The first child is a little boy. He passes by so quick I don't get a good look at him but he seems to be around five or six. Then, a little girl squeals at the boy 'I'm gonna get you!' as she runs down the stairs. I get a good look at this girl. She must be about seven or eight, with a long dress that comes to her mid calf. When she runs down the stairs she doesn't have to worry about lifting her dress like I do. And, her black lace-up boots make a loud thud on the wood staircase as she chases after him. They aren't our children, and we're a little annoyed that they are with us. My husband says something about them always misbehaving and yells after them to be careful.

"When we reach the top of the stairs, we turn left to go back to the front of the house. I look in some of the rooms upstairs, but my husband is behind me pushing me to see our room. It's at the front of the house. If you are in the street looking at the house, it's the window on the top right, over the living room. So, I go into the room and find that it's nice—not huge by today's standards or anything but it must have been pretty big back then. Based on the clothes and some other dreams I've had, I'm pretty sure this is the turn of the century, early 1900s.

"When I walk into the room, there is a large window, a double window to my right facing the front of the house. I walk over and look out. Over to the left is a large tree in the side of the yard. Looking below, I notice that we're close to the street. I look out across the street where some kind of construction appears to be going on. I then look to my right and know that there's a park in that direction, even though I can't see it. I'm excited and *really, really* happy.

"Then I feel my husband, who's still behind me, wrap his arms around me. I stand up straight and he turns me around. As soon as I'm face to face with him, I realize that he's the same one from the train honeymoon dream. I almost wake up, when I hear myself say 'not in front of the children'. I pull back to see his face one last time before he kisses me and, gazing down at me, deep down into my eyes, says 'Don't worry. I'm remembering too.' Of course, that throws me out of my deep sleep and kind of freaks me out. I don't know what he meant by that."

"How sweet! He loves you so much. Don't stop dreaming about him, okay?" Brenda says.

"So, how does Brent feel about this fellow?" her dad asks.

"Brent knows about everything. Luckily, he's very open-minded and not jealous. And, it's the perfect affair, in my dreams. Completely innocent."

"Yeah, I guess so. This must be the same fella that

put you in a rumble seat after you got married. I always waited for him to come around."

"What are you talking about, Dad? I haven't had any dreams like that . . . although, I suppose rumble seats were big during the time of these dreams. Like I said, from the clothes, I'm guessing it's around the turn of the century", says Angela, bewildered by her father's new line of questioning.

"Turn of the century as in 1910s and 20s?" Luther asks.

"Yeah. I guess so. Why?"

"Have you already forgotten when you were little and we'd drag you around to all the car shows? You remember we had that 1940 Ford truck and 1950 coupe we fixed up? You were a little thing back then. Not much over seven I suppose."

"How could I forget! We always went to the car shows. You loved the ones from the 40s and 50s and I loved the really old turn of the century cars! You're right. What a weird coincidence."

"Well, do you remember the Golden Nugget Classic Car Show in Nashville? I think it was around 1977 or '78."

"No." Angela replied.

"Well I do. Let me tell you about it . . ."

Angela sits quietly in the back of the 1950 Ford Coupe all the way to the car show. She enjoys the springing action of the back seat and the looks from admiring drivers they pass on the way to the show. Her father loves any model car from his childhood, 1950s and 60s. He has a particular affinity for the 1960s Corvettes but never has had the money to buy one. Instead, he satisfies his antique car needs by rebuilding classic cars of the 1950s. This is his passion. Angela likes cars from the 1950s and has grown to admire the early Corvettes as well. She likes their impression of speed, luxury and a modern car design all rolled into one. But, unlike her father, Angela's passion is for the older cars—older as in turn of the century, 1900 to 1930. Angela, only seven years old at the time, rarely gets the chance to see these cars but she loves them.

After a two-hour drive, Angela and her family finally arrive at the show and begin to look around. Brenda, normally bored at these events, brings a picnic lunch for them to enjoy later in the afternoon. If she gets bored walking around, she can always return to the car to set up the picnic in the large grassy open area next to their assigned parking spot.

The cars are parked in parking areas according to the decade in which they were introduced. Her father takes his parking assignment and drives the family over to the 1950 lots. Angela is surprised to see so many other cars looking like their own. Rows of Fords, both trucks and cars line the rows. Their owners line up with soft cloths to wipe clean the dirt and bugs from their latest drive or tow. Angela can't help but think they look like dog owners at a dog show, petting their prized possessions. She gets out and starts walking the lots with her parents.

After hours of looking at restored cars from the 1950s and 1960s, Angela is bored. Her father has spoken to every car owner in this section. She is hot and tired. "Mom, when are we going to my section?" she asks, as they patiently wait while her father discusses the finer points of chrome with yet another car owner.

"Just a minute honey. I think we're almost finished over here. We've looked at every one of these cars. The map says your cars are a close walk, so we'll make him go there next, okay?"

"Okay," Angela whispers, letting go of her mother's hand to fix one of her ponytails.

Luther finally finishes his discussion and agrees to see the older model cars, which he knows are always his daughter's favorite. He has only been into antique cars for two years, and his daughter, then five, had immediately taken to his hobby. He enjoyed having her along at the car shows. He felt like it was another thing he could share and teach her. But Angela's obsession with turn of the century cars was odd. He never cared for them, restored them or studied anything about them. Angela however always seemed to know quite a bit about them somehow. She loved them so much that Luther knew if she didn't save them for last, he'd never get her away from them to see his own favorite cars. Although Angela's older cars are rarely at his car shows, he knows there will be many here today, as a large section of the parking lot map has been reserved for them.

When they arrive at the appropriate section of the park with the older 1910-1930 cars, Angela is overwhelmed. She has never seen so many cars from this time period in one area. Most of the smaller car shows do not have these cars and she usually leaves disappointed. Today would not be one of those days.

She grabs her father's hand and pulls him towards the rows of old cars. As before, her father begins talking to the car collectors and owners of each car they examine. Angela does not stand with her mother and wait for him to finish talking this time. She looks over and inspects the cars, inside and out, tiptoeing to see the interiors and admiring headlights and paint jobs.

The owner of one car, Mr. Dempsey, takes notice in Angela's curiosity and comments to her father, "How great your little girl likes cars."

"Yeah. She always makes me come over to the classic cars. I only work with the later models, but this little one always insists . . . and you know how little girls can be!"

Mr. Dempsey smiles and turns his attention to Angela who is now opening the already cracked door, peering into his 1934 Ford Model A. "Do you like that?" he asks.

"Yes sir" she answers, "but I like the model Ts better, especially the ones with rumble seats."

Mr. Dempsey is a little taken back by her remark. He chuckles, "Do you really? Do you even know what a Model T looks like?"

"Sure. There's a speedster over there." She looks back to her left and points to a Ford Model T speedster. There are several here. But yours is a Model A, not T." Mr. Dempsey looks at Angela's father in disbelief.

"She knows the difference between models?"

"Yes" her father chuckles. "She can also tell you the years. I don't know how she does it. I couldn't identify the difference to save my life!"

Mr. Dempsey goes over to Angela and asks, "so, what year is this Model A?"

She looks the car over and concludes, "I'm not real sure. It's early 30s. I'm better at guessing the older Model T years. The Model A's are so much newer. They're harder for me to guess."

"So much newer?" Mr. Dempsey remarks in a bewildered tone, laughing. "What an odd thing to say!" He then calls over to his friend who is tending a car three spaces down, "Hey Clyde, get over here. You gotta see this."

A tall, overweight man slowly strides over to Mr. Dempsey, Angela and her father. He takes the pipe out of his mouth, looks at Mr. Dempsey and says, "whatcha got here?"

Mr. Dempsey kneels down next to Angela, places one hand on her back, points to Clyde's car and says "Do you see that car over there? That's Clyde's car. What kind of car is it?"

"It's a 1921 Packard," she answers simply, wondering why Mr. Dempsey is asking her instead of Clyde.

"Well, I'll be doggone!" Clyde replies. "How did you know that?" He asks her. Angela shrugs her shoulders as her father gleams with pride.

"How about that one?" Clyde says as he points to another car.

"1915 Studebaker," she replies. They gasp and invite other friends to watch in amazement. She responds each time with great accuracy.

Mr. Dempsey tells his friends, "This is amazing! She can not only tell the make and model. She can tell the difference between years! How can she do that? I've never seen anything like that in my life!" He looks over at Angela's father "Mister. That is one smart little thing you've got there!" Her father smiles and thanks Mr. Dempsey for his generous comments.

Another man named Darryl, noticing the small crowd, walks up to investigate. "What's going on here Clyde?" he asks. Clyde relays the last fifteen-minute questioning of the seven year old.

"Well, let's see what she has to say about mine," he

says as he approaches the center of the circle. "Do you see that blue car over there? The one by the pole? That's my car."

Angela looks over to the pole and is immediately awestruck by the most beautiful car she has ever seen. "Daddy look! Mama!" she yells as she points towards Darryl's car. She looks back up at Darryl, her eyes wide with excitement. "That is so pretty! Can I look at it?"

"Sure" he answers "But first tell me what kind of car it is."

"It's a Cadillac Roadster! Around 1918!" she yells excitedly. Feeling her heart skip a beat, Angela runs over to the car, leaving all the men with their mouths open in disbelief. "And," she announces to the group once by the car's side, "it has a rumble seat!"

Angela runs her small hand along the side of the car then steps back to get a complete view of it. It is cleaned to perfection, well kept and loved. The rumble seat, a trunk that opens to reveal an extra seat, is opened. She looks at Darryl, and reading her mind he asks, "would you like to sit in it?"

"Yes! Thank you so much sir!" she says as he swings her up, over and onto the rumble seat.

She looks around, eager to show the world she is seated in the lap of luxury. She closes her eyes and wishes she could stay seated here for the entire car show. She doesn't want to leave but knows she will have to eventually. Her mother looks on, arms crossed with a smile on her face. Her father is still talking to the group of men a few cars away.

Her eyes fill with excitement as she feels the tight leather of the seat. She closes her eyes and imagines herself riding down the road, the wind in her hair, the seat's springs bouncing her gently up and down.

"Mama, look!" she says, on the verge of tears looking over at her mother. "This is where you ride when you get married!"

November 2001, was the worst month in Angela's life. She was completely consumed with her first real trial. A corporation her firm represented, Declie International, was being sued by one of its former employees, Ms. Babcock, for wrongful termination. Ms. Babcock, a fifty-year old secretary, apparently discovered that the CEO and her boss, Mr. Weintrop, were undercutting the business and its stock by trading information with another corporation—its primary rival in the manufacturing technology field. Poor Ms. Babcock made the mistake of sending a complaint letter to the FTC, only to have it rerouted back to her boss for further investigation. In hindsight, she should have known better. The government has a terrible track record of returning squeal mail.

The trial was scheduled for the first of November and numerous attempts to settle were thwarted by the greed and ignorance of both sides. Angela and her associates represented the corporation and expected to settle early on in the game. So, it was a disappointment to have to finally go to trial. Nonetheless, she looked at it as a great opportunity to learn from peers and sharpen her oral skills.

A little known fact in the real world is that law firms are abuzz twenty-four/seven when trials are looming, and with each hour that passes, the client is billed an enormous amount of money for each attorney working on their case. Late night pizzas delivered to weary attorneys through cracked conference room doors become the prisoners' only solace as they brainstorm the method to their escape.

"All we have to do is get Riley on the stand and she'll back up everything Weintrop said," announces John, their lead attorney on the case.

"I disagree," says Angela as she gets up to pour another glass of juice. "This is all wrong. You know our client is guilty and I don't think our star witness, Ms. Riley, is reliable or credible."

"Why do you say that?" John asks, irritated that she would challenge him in any way.

"Because she's doin' Weintrop" Angela says simply.

"Where did you get that from?!"

"From the deposition. It was obvious. The minute she started talking I knew. It's been going on for a while too. And, she's trouble. She's jealous of his wife."

"That's ridiculous! We don't have time to strategize based on your hunches! Randall and I were both there and we didn't get any of that! Did you Randall?"

Randall sheepishly shakes his head no.

Linda, the only female partner at the firm interrupts. "Shut up, John. Give her chance. Angela, explain why that would be bad."

Angela stands in front of her chair, leans forward, and directly addresses John. "All I'm saying is that we're putting too much confidence in one witness. She's going to turn on you on the stand. She's not reliable. Even if you think my theory is full of shit, you have to recognize it's a dangerous strategy to place all your eggs in one basket. And letting the jealous lover of a married man hold that basket is suicidal to our case."

The phone rings, splitting the tension in the room. It's Richard, the firm's negotiator in the case. He is placed on a speakerphone, arranged in the center of the conference table. "A settlement has been reached! You can all go home now! It was the wildest thing. Come to find out, Weintrop and Riley had a thing going. Weintrop did something to piss her off and she promised to slam him on the stand. She told him Ms. Babcock would now be in his pants because she'd own 'em! So, of course he thought it would be better for the company to settle." Richard laughs and everyone else is silent, shocked at the confirmation of Angela's observation.

"Are you still there?" He asks.

"Yes Richard, we are. Thank you for all your hard work and the good news," Linda says as she reaches across the table to disconnect the speakerphone.

John sneers across the table at Angela. "What are you, psychic or something?"

"No." She answers unfazed by his rudeness, "I just pay attention."

Now confident, Randall says, "Angela, I'm looking at you and I have to ask, how did you know?"

She grins, cocks her head to one side and replies, "Randall, I'm looking at you and I have to ask how you didn't know. We are paid good money to pay attention." She gathers her papers, cleans her pizza scraps and heads to the door. For the first time in a month, everyone will sleep.

Brent is already asleep when Angela quietly climbs into bed. She is so tired she doesn't even bother to take off her silk blouse as she collapses on the pillow in complete exhaustion.

The cellar is dimly lit. Angela holds her crisp white apron in front of herself, filling it with potatoes from a crate on the floor. "They always make me come down here to get things. Ugh, I'm going to soil my apron again!" she exclaims. The weight of every potato delivers feelings of injustice and inferiority to her veins.

After filling her apron, Angela ascends to the kitchen where two of her sisters are waiting for her. The skinny sister is bent over the counter snapping pole beans into a large bowl and turns to give her a little smile, reading her mind, partly sympathizing with her chore. The kitchen is narrow but appears larger than it really is due to the sunlight pouring though windows. The windows are small half windows that are in front of the sink and over the counter to its right—two windows, open to the afternoon air. She is in the back part of the house.

Her larger sister is in front of the sink washing and peeling potatoes. Everything about her exudes her personality. She is strong, smart, dominating and older than Angela. She requests the potatoes and makes no apologies for soiled aprons. "She is a bully," Angela silently proclaims. Angela places the potatoes on the counter beside her sister just before her vision becomes cloudy.

She looks out the window and the scene begins to fades. Angela understands her visit is complete but is frustrated by the interruption. Time unfolds itself and drops her back into the place she considers her present home. Her silk blouse is still on, Brent is sleeping soundly by her side and Baghi is still on the floor.

Liz Carpenter had made the decision to move to Atlanta to be closer to her best friend Angela only one week before. Having begged Liz to move closer since they graduated law school in Miami, Angela was thrilled with the new turn of events. Liz's family lived in an area of the country that provided little to no opportunity for upcoming lawyers, so Atlanta offered great opportunity for her. Liz, a beautiful tall, brown haired, blue eyed beauty with a fabulous figure, quickly found a job, rented an apartment, and became active in her local Catholic church. Her down-to-earth, outgoing, kind personality helped her transition from one town to another easily.

Like most best friends, Liz and Angela complemented each other. They were sisters by choice rather than birth, and took great pride in holding each other together during the most difficult of times, such as getting through law school and studying for the bar.

Angela picks up the phone and calls Liz at her new apartment. Angela's voice does not hide her nervousness. "Liz, I have to come over now. Please tell me you don't have plans and you're not busy. I'll help you unpack or something. I know you don't start that new job until Monday."

"What's wrong with you?" Liz asks. "Of course you can come over. I was just going through some boxes. Do you still have the directions I gave you?"

"Yes. Great. I'll see you in a minute." Angela hangs up the phone and walks out of her office.

Angela follows the directions to Liz's new apartment, located just minutes from her parent's home. When she pulls into the driveway, Liz is at the front door eagerly awaiting her arrival.

"Oh, Liz! It looks great in here!" Angela exclaims as she peeks around the partially opened front door. "I love this new couch. Did you get that here, or bring it with you?" Angela asks, giving her best friend a hug.

"That was my grandfather's. He made it out of his

own bare hands . . . out of wood grown on his land in Minnesota . . . Isn't it beautiful? Mom had it shipped to me when he passed last summer."

"It really is incredible. I'm so glad you're finally here," Angela says, hugging Liz one more time.

"And I'm so glad to be here! So, cut it all out and tell me what's wrong with you. What's so important that you would just skip work this morning? Do you want something to drink? I just made some tea if you'd like. We have so much to catch up on," Liz says as she leads Angela to her new brightly lit, simple kitchen. Boxes are everywhere and it takes Liz a few minutes to search for tea glasses while Angela sits at the kitchen table.

"Well. I need to tell you something but, I really need you to be open-minded. And, I'm afraid I'll also have to swear you to secrecy," Angela says slowly and deliberately, noting every movement on Liz's face.

"You've got it. What's wrong?"

"I'm being haunted . . . Not by a ghost or anything scary like that! Just . . . well, I'm having some dreams and I think they're all related. They are me, but they aren't my life . . . at least not this one. Hell! I don't know what they are."

"Explain it. Tell me the dreams" Liz says, leaning toward her friend with great concern.

"Well, they're like movies, except, I get to see everything from the leading person's role. But, I don't have any control over what happens or who I see. I'm just there, in her body, as a spectator . . . Well, I'm in her body, but it feels like mine. So, I'm a spectator that has access to her thoughts, feelings, emotions, love, anger, everything. And I only get bits and pieces of the movie. I'm constantly being thrown in the middle and then yanked out of the scene. So, I never get a complete story. It's absolutely nuts," Angela explains.

"How long have you had these dreams?" Liz asks.

"Three years, on and off."

"Three years? Wow! And you are remembering them?"

"Crystal clear."

"Tell me all about them." Liz says with interest.

"How about I tell you about them, then email you hard copies for safekeeping?"

"Whatever you need."

Burden of Proof

The stars are particularly bright as Angela drives home on a late spring night. A light breeze caresses her hair as she approaches the front door of her house. Life has fallen into a pleasing harmony over the past few months and Angela feels a great peace and pride over her decisions in life. She is thankful for her work, which has slowed to a tolerable pace. She is thankful for her home and her family. She is thankful for the view of the moon and stars her house in the suburbs provides her. She never feels she purchased a parcel of land. She purchased a view of the heavens.

Before going to bed that night, Angela does something she doesn't often do; she prays. She wants God, or whoever might be listening, to know she's grateful for all she has been given. She knows she's privileged to have her life and experiences and to be surrounded by beautiful supportive people. Angela was never comfortable asking God to give her what she wanted, even as a child. So instead, she decides to say thanks and adds a sincere "let me know if there's anything I can do for you in return . . ."

Angela's thoughts quickly turn from her present contentment with her life to the characters in her dreams. It's been over a year now since her last dream.

She misses them and their surroundings and the way they make her feel. Somehow, she belongs to these people, places and time. Somehow, she has left them behind. She finds it difficult at times to live her daily life and deal with their absence in secret. She can only smile, continue to work and move about in this world and time as though she belongs. Underneath it all, she's grieving and thinking the entire time of her other family, her other home. It has to stop. It's beginning to take over. She decides to meditate once more before settling into bed. She needs to clear her mind and leave this family behind once and for all.

Angela rests quietly on her bed and imagines her muscles relaxing, bathed in a rich, warm and safe white light. Her muscles give way, her face tingles as her mind is set free. She finds herself in a tunnel. Her body is traveling though the tunnel at lightening speeds, even though she feels no acceleration. The tunnel moves around her, already sure of her destination. It's as if she has made this journey over a thousand times, recognizing paths of joining tunnels as they race by. She is filled with joy. At the end of the tunnel, her soul emerges into a park.

The park is large and manicured. The songs of birds overhead echo through the warm breezes and onto Angela's ears, her eyes closed. Even though there are benches behind her, she prefers to sit in the grass. She is seated with her legs out to her side. She grins and opens her eyes. In front of her no more than ten feet away is her daughter.

A smile sweeps over her face and her body warms as she watches her with great delight. Like any mother, she admires her daughter's grace and beauty, even though she appears to be no older than one year. She is playing with a blade of grass, examining and turning it over with her round healthy fingers as if it were something to which we should all devote such great attention.

Behind her, Angela is relieved to see a small iron fence separating the park from the sidewalk and road. "How great that they've put up that little fence. I don't have to worry about her and the street." On the other side of the street is a row of Victorian houses with beautiful front porches and gables. She admires the architecture while breathing in the smell of freshly cut grass.

The park is peaceful and happy. She considers it quiet even though she can hear the happy voices of older children playing behind her. Her thoughts turn to her husband, who should be arriving at any moment from work. She loves to meet him here in the park. These thoughts are running through her head as she looks to her right at a portion of the sidewalk blocked by a large bush. Her husband emerges from behind the bush with a smile on his face.

When Angela sees her husband her dream becomes lucid. Once again, the man from her train dream is before her. She is relieved to be back with him again and in response, her mind sends signals to her body demanding she not wake up from this dream. She feels her voice call out to her daughter who is still playing in the grass, although now seated, "Come on Greta. Daddy is here." Her body rolls awkwardly forward to attempt to stand. Angela feels a pregnant belly inhibiting her body's movement. She fights away consciousness.

She tries to ignore the pregnant belly and concentrates on the name her mouth has just spoken. "I can know my name," she thinks apart from her dream. Determined to know more, Angela demands, "What is my name?" Out of nowhere, a voice sounding like her own replies "Francine Donovan". She looks over to her husband, now completely in front of the bush with his arms outstretched and a smile on his face. With new-found confidence, she demands to know, "What is his name?" as a cloud of Angela's consciousness begins to cloud his image.

He comes closer and his face becomes clear again, "Claire" she hears a voice say just as clearly as it named Francine Donovan.

"No," Angela says in her dream, fighting the present, "that's a girl's name. What is his name? Please!" she calls out in desperation. "Cal" she hears in response. She awakens just as Cal is starting to kiss her on the cheek.

Disoriented, Angela's body fights its way out of the dream. She leaps out of bed, her eyes still unable to focus, and reaches for her dusty dream notebook she has hidden behind her bed. She takes out the pen she has included with her notebook and begins frantically writing down the names she has just heard in the order received. She writes:

GRETA
FRANCINE DONOVAN
CAL (CLAIRE?)

Angela stares at the list, bewildered. "Where did that come from? I can't believe I could see her so clearly. And, I was pregnant! Oh God . . . my imagination has really run wild." She places her pen into her journal, places it behind her bed and goes back to sleep. Now that her dream family has names, she thinks she will be able to finally say goodbye.

May 30th is an ordinary spring morning as Angela drives out of her garage, waves at her neighbor, and makes her way in to work. She isn't expecting anything out of the ordinary.

Arriving at the office early, Angela is determined to catch up on her work. Sandra isn't there yet, and to her dismay, her computer is also apparently half asleep and moving really slowly. Angela needs her morning tea and some breakfast.

She heads to the lobby sundry shop. The small, short man behind the counter wears overalls and a plaid shirt and greets his first customer of the day as he finishes placing fresh donuts in a glass case. "Mornin' Angela."

"Morning Freddy. You got any muffins this morning?"

"Sure 'nuff! Fresh as can be. Just picked 'em up. And you know I got your favorite, banana nut," he proclaims as he proudly holds up the muffin.

Angela takes the muffin and smiles "You're the best Freddy. What would I do without you? Is the tea ready yet? Fresh brewed right?"

"Of course."

Angela returns to her office with her tea and muffin to find her computer finally awake and ready to work. But Angela is distracted and cannot stop thinking about her dreams, even though work is piled up next to her desk. She looks around the room, down at her keyboard and says to herself mischievously "Okay. Twenty minutes and no more!"

Angela logs onto the Internet and goes to a search engine. She feels ridiculous as she types in "F-R-A-N-C-I-N-E D-O-N-O-V-A-N" and hits enter. Pages of possible combinations of "Francine" and "Donovan" appear on the screen. She quietly laughs at herself, amused that she would choose to kill some early morning work time in this way. For fun, she starts clicking on links, amazed by the variety of information she finds. She goes to another search engine and types in the same request.

She considers the wealth of information she has from the dreams. Most of the information is highly personal however, and she doubts any genealogy web page will be able to verify even half of what she knows from the dreams. The most validation she could hope for is confirmation that her Francine and Cal actually existed, lived at the turn of the century and had at least two children, the oldest a girl.

She figures, "what do I have to lose?" and starts taking the links that refer to genealogy research and finding lost loved ones. As she scrolls down the search site, a website catches her eye "Gene's Genealogy Guide". Gene's web page is linear, filled with names all linking to additional information. Angela is impressed by his organized approach and notices that he provides citations for his information along with a search engine for his website.

Again, she types in the name "Francine Donovan" and hits enter. To her surprise, there is a hit. She presses the name Francine Donovan, who lived at the turn of the century. The link takes Angela to an additional web page within Francine's database information. The new page says:

> Francine Donovan: Born Jan. 31, 1895 Lexington, KY USA. Death Feb. 25, 1923 (Calvary Cemetery)
> Father: Charles Michael Donovan
> Mother: Margaret Corrigan
> Spouse: Augustine Klair Weitzel
> Married: Apr. 22, 1919 (St. Paul's)
> Children: 1) Margaret Elizabeth Weitzel: born March 17, 1920 Lexington,KY USA. Death Feb. 29, 1976.

2) <u>Charles Jerome Weitzel:</u> born June 3, 1922. Lexington, KY USA. Death Nov. 14, 1968.

Angela's excitement quickly turns to frozen terror. "She was married to Claire . . . K-L-A-I-R, not C-L-A-I-R-E. Oh my God—And Margaret Elizabeth must be my Greta?" Angela feels her sanity unravel and settle into a pile at her feet. Strands of reason and reality are scattered about the floor leaving her with only a vision on a computer screen. Her vision is fixed and her speech silenced. She doesn't think she can move. She no longer feels her feet.

Angela moves her cursor to the entry of Augustine Klair Weitzel. The screen changes and more information appears. Augustine Klair Weitzel was born on January 31, 1887. Died in Lexington, Kentucky in 1936. Census reports attached to his record indicate that in 1900 he was a bartender. In 1910 and 1920 he worked as a salesman in wholesale groceries. In 1930, seven years after his wife's death, he was working as a waiter in a restaurant. The address of the married couple at the time of his first child's birth is listed as: 207 Woodland Avenue.

Angela scans back through the information, noting that Francine was only twenty-eight years old at the time of her death. Her son was nine months old. Her daughter had just turned three. She felt grief over the children's loss and couldn't imagine the pain and suffering Klair endured. The little girl from the park whom she called Greta grew up without a mother while baby Charles was abruptly torn from his mother's breasts for an eternity.

Inexplicable feelings of guilt sweep over Angela as the pit of her stomach begins to twitch. Her dreams of

Francine had multiplied the year Angela herself turned twenty-eight.

Francine was first generation Irish from her father, second from her mother. Klair was first generation German from his father. Angela's heritage is Irish and German.

Francine's father and many of her brothers worked for the railroads. They were railroad engineers at the time of the various census reports according to this website. That would explain Francine's thoughts on the train about her family's obsession with train safety. One of her brothers was actually a fireman for the railroad.

But, Angela keeps coming back to one fact: both of Francine's children are gone. Everyone in her direct family is now dead. Passing through the family pages, Angela quickly realizes there is no one still alive who knew Francine; no one to care that she has surfaced again in Angela's dreams. Angela struggles to find purpose to her dreams. If they carry a message for someone, who should or could hear it? They are all six feet under, pushing up daisies.

Suddenly, a calm surrender overcomes Angela's spirit as she stares in awe at the names on the computer. She would eventually understand that perhaps she had been chosen to receive this wisdom, placed in a position to provide proof of some supernatural realm her past religion forbid her from entering. She feels privileged, humbled, and grateful. She feels undeserving and vows not to screw it up—that is, if her dreams could actually be validated.

She knows she should not run away. She has to return this favor bestowed on her by the heavens. She would have to proceed cautiously and prove that the remaining facts of her dreams are in fact true and related to this family. She believes with every thread of her body that they are. She gathers all of her strength and after what seems like four lifetimes, hits the print button on her browser.

Angela knows the dreams she has experienced could be a variety of things. In her favorite television show, *Unsolved Mysteries*, she's watched about people who claim to spontaneously recall their past lives. She once saw a program about dead loved ones visiting their relatives in dreams. But, as far as she could tell, unlike those cases, there was no connection to Francine or Francine's ancestors in those dreams. There were no messages to relay or family mysteries to solve. There was no communication, only occupation of Francine's life.

Could she be remembering a past life? Could she be communicating with the dead spirit of Francine? Was this how it happened for mediums? She was absolutely clueless. Her strict fundamental Christian upbringing offered no alternative explanation apart from instant and certain damnation, a concept she no longer believed in at all. She knew she would have to do some research before drawing any conclusions.

Angela decided to spend a Saturday morning in a large New Age bookstore, very unlikely and unfamiliar territory for her. Angela dressed conservatively— even if she was one of "them" now she wasn't prepared yet to look the part—and quietly left the house so as not to wake Brent. The day before, she had carefully selected her bookstore, consulting the Yellow Pages and calling to inquire about the size of their selections. She settled on what proclaimed to be the largest metaphysical bookstore in Atlanta, The Wish Fulfilling Tree.

Angela pulls into its parking lot only ten minutes after the store's opening. With notebook and pen in hand, she explains to the kind man behind the counter that she is doing some research and asks if he would mind her taking notes or asking questions.

"Certainly not. Just ask me anything and I'll be glad to help out. Have you seen our new arrivals?" he asks kindly. Dressed comfortably in jeans and a maroon t-shirt, his smooth voice and calm manner immediately comfort Angela. She is sure his advice will be helpful. She considers telling him about her dreams for a split second, but then quickly decides against it.

"No. I'm really just here for a specific theme of book. Mainly just talking to dead people and/or reincarnation stories," she responds frankly.

"Well, they're over there to your right. We've got quite a selection. Buddhist books have quite a bit of general information. But, if you're just looking for stories, I'd check into some of Brian Weiss' books. Those are real popular these days."

Considering his suggestion, Angela makes her way to the correct area of the bookstore. She picks out one of Dr. Weiss' books first. As far as she can tell, this Dr. Weiss guy is able to do past life regressions on his patients. They are taken from lifetime to lifetime, from scene to scene, and are eventually cured of all kinds of ailments as a result. As she thumbs through his cases, she is surprised by two things. One, that they never seem to get full names, if any at all. Two, they almost always remember their deaths. This does not settle well with her and she begins to feel sorry for his subjects, even though they appear grateful. "Who in their right mind would go get a regression just to remember a death?" she thinks to herself.

She reads on. Apparently, the subjects are viewing rather than experiencing what is happening to them. "That's a relief," she thinks to herself, "since they tend to be horribly tragic. But, they are very different from what I experience. Nothing he describes is similar to my dreams. No psychologist regressed or hypnotized me. I didn't have an out-of-body experience—I thought it was really me!" She reads on in disappointment, looking for some kind of similarity. She finds none. "They don't even remember their names." She shakes her head and puts the book back on the shelf.

Moving past more shelves, Angela is now intent on avoiding the psychologists who advertise they can muster up a past life faster than you can buy french fries at a drive-thru. She begins looking for books written by people who have actually realized that their own dreams or visions were past lives. Out of all the books in the largest metaphysical bookstore in Atlanta, she finds only two. She purchases them both, along with two other books on the general subject of reincarnation.

A 1996 study by the Department of Justice concluded that the number one cause of wrongful convictions in the United States was mistaken identification. Recent developments in DNA testing have led to more and more discoveries of mistakes made by witnesses forced to identify a person out of a line up. Innocent people have been sent to death row based on witness identification, only later to be exonerated by DNA evidence. It happens. And, Angela is very aware of this as she reads through the books she has purchased on reincarnation.

She can't help but be critical; it has been trained into her blood. She approaches each individual story of reincarnation as a juror with legal training. She sees no objective evidence, only subjective striking similarities between their recollections and another's life. "Circumstantial evidence," it's called in criminal cases. Examining every line of proof presented by each case, she analyzes every link of the evidence that has led the author to conclude he or she is in fact the reincarnation of a particular person.

Angela notices that these authors don't often get names. She finds no stories where they spontaneously recall their first and last name, the name of the husband and daughter. They are left with only some image of what they look like. Some actually look for photos of themselves in libraries or old family albums, searching for an identification to latch onto. She is shocked and disappointed. "How many of my ancestors have their photos in a library book?" "None" is the simple answer. "And how do the authors know what they looked like?" This question intrigues her. Her dreams have all been in the first person. She had no idea she was dreaming of someone else until she saw herself in the mirror on the train. If she had a lineup of Victorian women in front of her today, she knows she could not reliably identify the correct woman of her dreams. And, knowing how reliable human recall can be when confronted with line-ups, she is not impressed.

This, she concludes, is where most chains of proof break down. This is a real shame because she suspects some of these writers' memories, dreams and regressions are valid memories of another life. But, they become muddled and less credible by the victim's urgency for a validation. She realizes the same thing could happen to her. She could say, "Oh, I'm a Victorian woman traveling in a private train car in the United

States on my honeymoon," and start looking for women who match that description and had long dark hair. Eventually, she would find someone. Traveling by trains was common at the turn of the century and many new brides did it. Many of those new brides had long dark hair too. But that alone is not a validation. That is a coincidence. Once you identify one of those brides, you can't then go examining her life looking for similar factors on which to build your case. You must have a more stable foundation for the proof.

Returning home, she begins to plot her strategy. Angela takes these books as examples of what not to do. Pulling out the dreams she has emailed Liz, Angela sits at her kitchen table and begins to write on a legal pad. She makes two columns, marking one "Objective" and the other "Subjective." In the margin, she writes the titles she has given to each dream "The train dream; the wedding dream; potatoes; shopping for shoes, hotel, etc." She then painstakingly enters the objective, or hard, facts in the corresponding columns. These are facts such as her surroundings, the situation, conversations and clothes. Under subjective facts, she places emotions, things she knows from the dreams without reason, time periods, her age, and the feel of her body. Confirmation of these entries will be her proof. When something is verified, she will mark through it. If something contradicts that fact, she promises herself she will make an "x" mark next to it. And, she does.

Using the information from Gene's website, spread out before her, Angela begins her analysis. She happily places check marks by the names in the park dream, leaving the name "Greta" with a question mark, as it appears to be an unconfirmed nickname. Next to the house dream, she places a provisional "x". Census reports indicated Klair was a bartender in 1900, a grocery store salesman in 1920 (the year after their marriage), and a waiter in a restaurant in 1930. Angela doubts a grocery store salesman would be affluent enough to buy the house bought for her in the dream, or to be from a prominent family. Nonetheless, she would continue searching for more proof based on the names that matched the family of her dreams.

Angela paces back and forth in Liz's living room holding her proof sheet and copies of the dreams in email form. "This is how I want to go about it. Let me know if you see any holes. Be my devil's advocate." Liz, listening patiently on the sofa, is ready to take in Angela's presentation.

"I know this is going to sound weird. But, did you notice in the last dream I emailed you I got names?"

"Names? No, I haven't really looked at it yet."

"Well, I got the first and last name of the person I've been dreaming about off and on for the past three years."

"You're kidding me! What was her name?"

"Francine. Francine Donovan. And she was married to a man named Klair and she called her daughter Greta."

"That's amazing! How did you get that?"

"I just asked and I heard their names. That simple . . . while I was dreaming of course."

"You interrupted your dream to ask questions?"

"Yeah. Don't you ever do that? I'm always trying to control my dreams. I can't control these dreams at all, but I just found out I can ask questions!"

"Okay. You know that is *really* weird don't you?"

"All of this is weird, Liz. *Really* weird. Get this now. I was sitting around at work one morning trying my best to avoid work. I logged onto the Internet and started playing around looking for the names. I found them."

"What?" Liz's eyes widen, she sits up straight and scoots to the edge of the couch.

"I found them. The family. Her name is Francine Donovan and she is married to a Klair. K-L-A-I-R, not C-L-A-I-R-E like I wrote down in the park dream. It's his middle name. His first name is Augustine."

"Oh my God! That's incredible. Can I see?"

"Sure, here it is" says Angela as she hands her the printouts from Gene's Genealogy website.

Liz looks over the information, speechless and overwhelmed. "So even though he's got a nice first name like Augustine, you're saying he went by his sissy middle name?" Liz takes a deep breath and looks up at Angela with her large, blank eyes. Angela nods her head affirmatively. Liz shakes her head incredulously, looks down at the papers and says, "This is big. This is really big Ang . I can't believe this. Do you know how big this could be? Do you really think it's them?"

"Duh! Of course I think it's them. There are some facts that are inconsistent. But how many couples in the world are named Francine and Klair? It has to be them!"

"So what are you going to do?"

"Well, that's why I'm here. I needed another attorney's opinion on burden of proof. What is my burden going to be?"

"It looks like you already have what amounts to a confession right here. They've fried many criminals in Sparky the electric chair on confessions alone."

"Yes, and some of them were innocent too. So,

what is the burden of proof for capital punishment cases? It's been so long since the bar."

"Beyond a reasonable doubt."

"That's it. That's what I'll have to require for myself."

"So how do you intend to go about proving this?"

"I think the only way would be to take a trip to Lexington, Kentucky where Gene says this family lived. I've never been there before or done genealogy research, but surely I can use my legal research skills to find anything and everything on these people in public records."

"True. I guess it would be all be in the library or the courthouse."

"There's also a church named St. Paul's. Maybe they have records too."

"So how do you show you didn't know all this stuff before you had the dreams?"

"The emails and my journals. Of course, dates in journals could be forged. So, that's why I emailed them all to you earlier. Emails have the dates and times put on them by independent servers."

"Ohhhh . . . that's good. That's really good!"

"Thank you. Now, there's another not so good reason for it too. I don't trust myself. Once I learn things about these people, the lines become skewed between information drawn from the dreams and information drawn from research. I have to do a lot of work to make sure that line remains sharp. That's why I've made this chart, dividing the subjective from objective facts. The dreams I sent you contained mostly objective facts. This is all dated and I am not allowing myself to touch it anymore. That's why I sent it to you. For safekeeping."

"Don't worry, I'll hold onto it. I still have all the emails you sent."

"Print them out, put them up. Copy them to disk. Make sure they don't get destroyed or lost.

"Okay."

"And, one more thing. Please don't tell anyone just how crazy your best friend has become."

Liz laughs, falls back onto the couch and places her hands behind her head. "You are one crazy and brave woman. Can you imagine what your colleagues would say if they knew what you planned on doing?"

"I can imagine. That's why they aren't going to know. I need to keep my credibility, and my job." Angela's heart fills with an odd mixture of excitement and caution. She whispers the names over and over to herself, sure she has found an identity to her dreams. She isn't sure what is going on, or what will happen to her. The information in the dreams and on the Internet could prove she was somehow psychic or just plain crazy. Either way, she fears she'll end up alone, diagnosed with a mental illness, and laughed at all the way to the psychiatrist's chair. At a minimum, she's in love with people she has never met who happen to have been dead for decades.

The Scheduling Order

Angela is in her office bright and early at 8am when the phone rings. It is Liz.

"Hey. You want to meet for breakfast?"

"Sure. I have a deposition later this morning and that would be on the way. See you in 10 minutes? Same place?"

"Deal," says Liz, "see you soon."

Angela hangs up the phone and picks up her brief-case and coat.

Angela and Liz meet whenever they can for breakfast. Since law school, time has begun to run faster and moments with friends are scarce. Liz works in a law firm about ten blocks away from Angela's doing mostly employment and contract law cases. She's a good attorney and enjoys the friendly contact she has daily with blue collar workers. They remind her of her family, and her heart bleeds at least twice a day.

Angela starts out her office door and realizes that Sandra, her secretary, has arrived. "Good morning, Sandra. Are we having a good day? Did Milton finally get his stuff moved out?" she asks.

"Yeah. Everything but that mutt. They're just alike you know. They snuggle up and then piss on you." Sandra laughs as she arranges the papers on her desk.

110

"Listen," Angela announces to Sandra. "I'm heading out for a breakfast appointment. Then, I have a deposition at 10:30. I should be back by two. Okay?"

"Sure. I'll page you if anything urgent comes up."

"Fine. Thanks." Angela turns and heads towards the front door of the firm, which leads to the floor elevators. Suddenly, Max, the new associate she has befriended, appears from an adjoining hall and blocks her way out the front doors. Nervously, Max says "Good Morning Angela. I was hoping you could do me a favor today and review this brief. I just completed the intentional tort argument and I have to turn it in to Carl before we file it"

"I'm sorry Max. I'm running late. I can't do it right now, but if you leave it with Sandra I'll review it when I get back. Would four this afternoon be too late?" she asks impatiently, leaning around him with full intentions of making it out of the door with little else to say.

"Sure! Perfect," Max sighs with audible relief.

The morning air outside the office is brisk and pleasant. People are walking with coats on, their hands tucked firmly in pockets. The birds enjoy the morning and bask in the leftover bagel someone has tossed to the ground. An old man huddles in the corner of the building on the ground, hungry and escaping the wind that threatens to take away his last bit of warmth. She'll take him a cup of coffee on her way from the cafe to the deposition. He'll be grateful, thank her and drink down its warmth. The walk to the café is over before she knows it. Liz has already arrived and ordered their breakfast.

"I got your usual" she informs Angela as she makes her way to the table.

"Thanks! Ugh. I thought I'd never get out of there. That job is seriously interfering with my personal life,"

Angela laughs out loud while Liz fights the urge to choke on her coffee.

"I know what you mean," Liz says as she sips her coffee.

"After this," Angela explains, "I've got to go to a deposition at Tallman's."

"Tallman law firm?" Liz asks.

"Yep."

"Oh, she's good. Do you have a good case?"

"Yes. Thank God. And her client is a real low life. Lucky for us, he lies about everything."

"It's your favorite kind of case then—catching liars!" Liz is amused that this is about the only pleasure Angela gets out of her job these days. She knows how Angela values honesty and hates it when people try to lie to her. She knows her friend has fired more than one client for dishonesty and admires her for pulling no punches when it comes to representing the corporate thieves of our society. Now that Angela is settled in, sipping her tea and having breakfast, Liz decides to break the good news.

"You are not going to believe where I have to go on business!" she says, eager to tell Angela, but wanting to throw in a little suspense. Angela guesses, "Spain? Italy?"

"No. Even better than that!"

"Better than those?" Angela is truly stumped.

Liz laughs. "How about Lexington, Kentucky?"

Angela is shocked by the news. She has been trying hard to repress memories of her dream family so she can lead a normal life. Today, she had made it all the way to breakfast without a hint of them. She was so proud of herself. But, this news was definitely good and welcomed, despite her efforts to distance herself temporarily from it all.

"You're kidding me? I'm so jealous . . . I don't know what to say." Angela pauses, looks over at her best friend, and lowers her voice. "You have to look them up. Will you have time? Can you?" She begs.

"For you, I'll make time."

"That would be so great. I just can't believe it! It doesn't look like I'll ever get to go with my schedule. But, you could help me out!"

Liz smiles and nods her head. "I was thinking I could start out by finding their graves. My schedule is crazy though . . . I probably won't have time for much more."

"Well," Angela says, "I'm pretty sure she was Catholic. Aren't you Catholics buried in your own separate cemeteries? Gene's website said they are buried in a placed called 'Calvary'."

"You never told me she was Catholic." Liz says as she motions for the waitress to bring over the bill.

"Well, I never said anything because it was a feeling I got in the church dream. I tried to keep the dreams I emailed you objective. I didn't see a big poster that said 'Hey, You! You're Catholic.' And, since I've never been Catholic, I thought it was a bit weird to recognize a feeling of being Catholic."

"So, how does it feel to be Catholic?" Liz asks amused at her friend's new perception.

"Well, kind of itchy . . . You know, Ms. Catholic woman! Seriously, it was kind of nice." They laugh together, pay the bill and make their way outside.

Liz finalizes her trip to Lexington, Kentucky and one week later is off the ground and on her way. Her itinerary is full, but she will make time to find the cemetery and take some pictures before she leaves. She goes over her agenda on the plane, looks out the window at the rolling countryside and knows she's almost there. She has trouble concentrating on the real purpose of her trip—business. Angela's memories of Francine and Klair have crept into her mind and sparked a sense of curiosity and adventure. Liz understands just how important this is to her friend, even if it is just a trip to a cemetery.

When she arrives, she secures her rental car and heads over to her hotel. Nearby, on her way to the hotel she sees a grocery store and decides to stop there. She is in desperate need of a good map and a disposable camera. After easily finding the camera and map, Liz begins her wait in the long checkout line. Before she reaches the counter, the lady behind her strikes up a conversation.

"So, you from out o' town?" Liz hears in a soft southern accent coming from behind. She turns around to see the smallest, sweetest grandmotherly figure.

"Yes. As a matter of fact I am. I'm just buying this map so I can find my way around." Liz answers.

"Oh. This ain't no big town, but we are mighty friendly. I hope you enjoy your stay," the lady says with a genuine smile on her face.

"Well thank you." Liz decides to take advantage of her kindness and ask for directions. "Say, would you happen to know where Calvary Cemetery is?"

"Calvary? No. I've never heard of that. Don't know where you might find that." With a soft smile, she turns to the man standing slightly behind her. "Chad, you ever heard of that?" she asks him. "No" he responds.

Just then, the lady that had just paid and walked out the door turns around and approaches Liz. "Mam, I was just listening to your conversation. I think I know where Calvary Cemetery is. Is that the old Catholic cemetery?" she asks Liz.

Without pausing, Liz answers "Yes, that's probably it". She immediately thinks of Angela's advice to look for a Catholic cemetery because she "felt" Catholic. It strikes her as odd that something so subjective about a dream could be correct. She takes down the directions from the lady, thanks her for her kindness and says goodbye to grandma and Chad.

The next day, Liz is in meetings all day. On purpose, she scheduled her return flight for the next morning so she would have all late afternoon and night to explore the city. When her meetings conclude, she gets into her rental car, spreads out the map and looks for the directions given to her by the grocery store lady. She drives down the two lane narrow streets, slowing down to read the signs. Finally, she sees the entrance to Calvary Cemetery and turns left in between two large stone columns holding up a large iron fence.

Liz pulls in front of a house that now serves as the office. The house is quaint and sits at the entrance of the cemetery. It is two-story, colonial style, with a large front porch. Liz climbs the creaking staircase and reaches for the front door. The door squeaks under her touch, announcing her arrival. Once inside, she is greeted by red carpets and a large staircase. A small, kind woman comes from another room, which has been converted into an office.

"Hello." Liz says, "I was wondering if you could help me find a gravesite." The woman motions her to a chair to sit down.

"Who are you looking for? I'll need first name, last name and date of death if you have it," she says to Liz.

"Well. I have that information. I'm looking for a

Francine Donovan, buried February of 1923. She was married to Augustine Klair Weitzel, who I also suspect is buried here." The lady hands Liz a sheet of paper and pen from her desk.

"You'll have to write these down for me. I'm not a great speller." She opens up a cabinet to Liz's right. Inside the cabinet are drawers of card indexes. She runs her finger along the faded cards on the outside and begins pulling out drawers.

"Donovan. I have a lot of Donovans, but no Francine." She closes the drawers, metal shrieking against metal.

"Weitzel. Here you go. I have Augustine Klair Weitzel, Francina Weitzel and a Charles Weitzel. Is that them?"

"Yes. I believe it is." Liz gets up and looks at the card the lady is holding. On the reverse side of Francine's card she notices an address: 315 W. Maxwell St. Before she can write it down the lady takes the card out of her hand, places it back into the drawer and locks the cabinet. Liz is taken aback by her brisk action, but soon realizes it's almost closing time for this lady. Liz is given specific instructions on how to find the gravesites and then walks out of the door whispering the address to herself. When she gets to the car, she scribbles down the address and sets out for the gravesite.

As her car enters the burial grounds, she is struck by the beauty and peacefulness of the cemetery. Placed along slightly rolling hillsides, it is covered by old trees that appear to spread their comforting arms over all who come there to mourn. But the trees are old and the mourners have long joined their loved one's sides under the embrace of the trees, tucked between their protective roots.

Most of the gravestones date back to the 1800s, but are remarkably well kept. Liz thinks to herself that as a

Catholic, she could only hope to be buried in such a wonderful place. It isn't long before she locates the gravesites that sit alongside the narrow road that winds it way past the markers. Liz sees Klair's gravesite first, with large letters under his name announcing he was "FATHER". She parks the car, gets out and walks closer. She laughs out loud as she stands in front of the tombstone and reads "A. Klair" sketched onto the tombstone. To her surprise, Angela was right. He did go by his middle name. Francine's gravesite is next to Klair's and announces "MOTHER". Francine's son, Charles, is on the other side of his mother's gravesite. Her daughter, Margaret Elizabeth, is not there.

Liz stands in front of Francine's and Klair's gravesites, crosses her arms, looks around to make sure she's alone and begins to speak out loud. "You're driving my friend crazy. I don't know what you are doing, but please finish soon and leave my friend alone." To her relief, nobody responds. She closes her eyes, bows her head, and says a quick Catholic prayer for the dead.

Liz picks up her sleek silver cell phone which glistens in the sun in sharp contrast to the dull gray weathered tombstones at her feet, and calls Angela, who is still in her office going over new evidence in a case. "Guess where I am?" she says.

"Cemetery?" Angela responds.

"Yep. I'm standing here looking at Francine and Klair's grave." A chill travels up Angela's back and back down again as she shifts in her office chair and firmly grips the phone.

"Well, tell them I said hello!" Angela says as she smiles and closes her eyes, choking away tears of excitement and envy.

Liz holds the phone out to her side, "Francine, Klair, Angela says hello."

"Well, they didn't say anything, but I'm sure they appreciate the recognition," Liz quietly laughs, knowing this is the strangest thing she's ever done.

"Listen. You were right. He went by Klair. His tombstone says A. Klair. Augustine isn't spelled out at all. I also got her address from the cemetery card. I'm going there after I take some pictures for you."

"Wow. And the house? Oh, I hope it's the same house from my dream. I already have an address from Gene's website. It's probably the same one. You call me as soon as you get there. I'm not going anywhere! Thank you so much!"

"You're welcome," Liz turns off her cell phone, takes some pictures, then makes her way back to the car.

Back at the car, she pulls out the map and quickly locates West Maxwell Street. It isn't very far away and she should have no trouble locating the house, if it still stands. She weaves her way through the tiny road, under the enormous trees, out of the cemetery and back onto the main road. After a few easy turns, she is on West Maxwell Street counting down the numbers on the businesses and few remaining old houses. As she nears her target, Liz notices a small deserted parking lot and pulls in.

Happily, she realizes that she has just parked in front of the address she is looking for, 315 West Maxwell Street. She starts to get out of the car to take some pictures when she sees a sign in the small front yard of the house: "*Shambhala Meditation Center.*" Liz's mouth drops wide open and she begins to laugh hysterically.

"This just can't be," she thinks to herself. "Angela is not going to believe this!" Liz sits in her car for a moment to allow the shock and amusement to wear off. She decides that since it is a business open to the public, she may as well go in and take a look. She gets out of the car, takes a quick picture and crosses the street to the front door. She slowly opens the front door because it still looks and feels like a private residence. In the front hall, she is greeted by a short, thin woman in a yellowed flower dress.

"Hello? Come on in. We're open. My name is Judy. How can I help you?" Liz pauses for a moment, looking over at a display with brochures.

"I'm new to the area. What exactly do you do here?" she asks.

"We provide instruction on meditation and have education seminars on Buddhism and religiously neutral themes as well." Judy responds.

"May I take some of these pamphlets?" she asks as she goes over to the pamphlets on the table. "Actually, could I have a few minutes of your time? I have some questions." Liz looks over at Judy, hoping for a positive response, still shocked she is standing in Francine's house with people meditating inches away from her in an adjoining room. "Sure." Judy responds.

"Well, you see" Liz nervously searches for words, trying to make it sound as normal as she possibly can. "I'm here because of my best friend. She's having dreams of a family that lived here in Lexington and they may have lived here, in this house. I'm in town and promised to look some things up for her. An address on a cemetery card led me here. It said she lived here when she died." She explains.

Judy looks at her a little strangely, shifts her feet, forces a smile and says, "Well, we don't include dream interpretations as part of our meditative practice or classes, but I suppose anything is possible." Judy pauses to measure Liz's reaction. Liz's silence begs for further explanations. "Would you like a tour of the house for your friend?" Judy suggests, "I see you have a camera. You're welcome to take pictures."

Liz perks up immediately, uncomfortable with the subject and eager to move on. Judy leads her up a stairway to the left of the front door. Liz struggles to remember the details of Angela's dream of her house, and begins looking for the large front windows. To her dismay, there are no large windows facing the front of the house, only small square windows. The house is simple, cozy and quaint, with its own southern flair. It has the requisite front porch, hardwood floors, wood trimming and a fireplace in the front parlor.

The living room and master bedroom are empty except for large red and yellow mats strewn across the floor. One downstairs window has been replaced with a stained glass window containing a large yellow circle. It reminds Liz of a smiley face and she fights the urge to draw two points for eyes and a happy smile when she passes by. Judy continues the tour outside, where they have created a beautiful garden. Liz is impressed with their work. She knows Angela will be happy they are keeping her house in order.

She thanks Judy for all of the time and information she has so willingly shared and makes her way back across the street to her car. Once in her car, she calls Angela, who's still at work nervously awaiting her call.

"Well, I just had a tour of the house." She announces once Angela answers the phone.

"No way! How? Where are you?"

"I took the last known address for Francine off the back of the cemetery card. It was 315 West Maxwell Street. And, now I'm here and I just had a tour."

"You have to tell me everything! Was it like my dream?" Angela asks, barely able to make a sentence from her excitement.

"Well, I couldn't find your big windows. And,

there's no big tree out front, but they've really kept it up nice. You won't believe what it is now!"

"Oh! Don't make me guess. What is it?" Angela asks

"The Shambhala Meditation Center," Liz shakes her head again in disbelief as she listens to her friend laughing hysterically on the other line. Once Angela recovers, she is eager for details.

Liz explains. "When you first come through the front door, there is a staircase to your left."

Angela interrupts. "Stop right there. That's not the house. Is the front door in the middle of the house?" She asks.

"No. It's on the left side if you're looking at it. It has a living room to your right and then upstairs there are a few rooms." Liz explains.

"No." Angela's tone goes somber. "That's not the house. Where is the park? There should be a park nearby. Do you see the park?"

"No. I haven't seen any parks around here. This road is pretty filled up. I've driven down some of it, but no park."

"Well, that's not the house. It doesn't fit the description from my dream. I don't think she ever lived there." Angela feels confused and disappointed. "What address do you have?"

"315 W. Maxwell."

"No. Gene's website said they lived somewhere else." She knows the cemetery card claims it was Francine's last known address, but she must be honest with herself that the description she is hearing is not consistent at all with her dream of the house.

Liz returns home, eager to share her notes, photocopies and pictures with Angela. Oddly, Liz's trip has done nothing but convince Angela that none of this can be resolved until she goes to Lexington on her own to do research. "Will you go back again? With me? I've never been there and could use your help." Angela begs Liz.

"Sure. I'll go back. It's a real nice city. We could drive up there. I think it would probably take us six or seven hours at the most. When would you want to go?"

"I'm not sure. Not now, it's too cold. Maybe in springtime. My trial should be over by March, so how about April?" she asks as she gets out her Palm Pilot. "How about the weekend of the 14th?"

"Is that Easter?" Liz asks.

"No. It looks like the week before," Angela says as she points to the date on the screen to make sure she doesn't have anything already planned.

"Palm Sunday," notes Liz, glancing at the calendar.

Angela asks, "Is that an important Catholic thing? Do you need to be with your family or in church?"

"No. Not necessarily. It's important, but not as big as Easter. We could always go to Mass at Francine's church. We have to go there anyway."

"True. That would be alright with me. So I'll put us down for a road trip the weekend of April 14th?"

"That's fine. It should be fun! That way, we'd only have to take Friday and Monday off work . . . make it a long weekend."

"Great!" Says Liz, "this should be different!"

"That's an understatement!" chuckles Angela. "Listen, If anyone asks, I'm not going to lie, I'm going to tell them I'm going to do genealogy research," Angela winks at her friend.

"Sure thing! I'll tell them the same."

PART II

My Old Kentucky Home

Weep no more my Lady.
We will sing one song for the Old Kentucky home . . .
For the old Kentucky home far away.

—Stephen C. Foster (Kentucky state song)

Southern Charm

"Do we have to go?" Angela asks as she pulls on the only cocktail dress she owns. "Can't we just stay home and eat pizza?" she begs, adjusting her red dress in the mirror. The long straight dress seductively clings to her curves, elegantly accentuating her feminine features. Brent's English professor is hosting a dinner party for the department and Angela has reluctantly promised to attend. Everyone who is anyone plans to be there, and she knows networking opportunities like these should not be missed.

"Do you not like my friends?" Brent asks, straightening his tie in the bathroom mirror and taking a step back to admire his wife in her red dress. "Well. They're nice and all . . . just a little stiff. I feel like I have to be fake around them."

"But you don't! Just be yourself," Brent suggests in a soft British accent that always calms his wife.

"I'm not sure that's the Angela they want to meet. Which Angela would you like tonight? The professional attorney over-educated Angela or the down home pass-me-some-more-Jack-Daniels-and-where-did-I-leave-my-shoes-Angela?"

"How about a little of both . . . with shoes?" he teases, wrapping his arms around her from behind and bending down to kiss her bare shoulder, his soft brown hair caressing her cheek.

"Ugh! You're so formal!"

"And you are such a mess!" he says, as he pats her on the rear and then goes to finish straightening his tie.

The drive to the party takes them down streets lined lusciously with overhanging oak and pecan trees. Behind the trees, nestled far into the woods, glimpses of stately mansions dot the horizon.

"How in the world do professors afford to live here?" she asks.

"They haven't always been professors," Brent replies.

Professor Jake Howard's home is situated far from the road and is a quintessential southern home. Stately Oak trees line the narrow paved driveway, which winds from the busy main road up to his quiet, tranquil home. The large Victorian manor sits on a hill, complete with wraparound porch and large white columns that whisper 'old money' to all those who pass between them. The brick façade is decorated by bands of wisteria and well kept ivy. Brent carefully positions their seven-year old humble sedan between the new Mercedes and Beamers lining the circular driveway at the door and around a beautiful ceramic fountain.

The atmosphere inside the home is no different. Decorated in the old turn of the century style, the beautiful foyer has a magnolia theme.

"Brent! So glad you could come," bellows Dr. Howard, the southern host with a New York accent. "And . . . wow! This must be Angela . . . So nice to finally meet you." Angela smiles and extends her hand to Dr. Howard, but, he turns away from her and wraps his arm around Brent's shoulder. "I'd like for you to meet Grant Ludlow. He's in from New York where he's just completed another screenplay. You must discuss your thesis with him." Dr. Howard turns Brent away from the foyer area, leaving Angela all alone and disgusted.

Shocked at his rudeness, she looks around. The southern charm of the décor was the only thing left to greet her, so she decides to help herself to a tour of the house. She looks up at some large paintings of people she's sure Dr. Howard doesn't know, then proceeds down a narrow hallway beginning behind the stairs. She peeks through a slightly opened door along the corridor. It appears to be a back entrance to the kitchen where three maids are busy preparing hors d'oeuvres. Their northern accents are sharp and unhappy. Angela opens the door wider and peaks in.

Behind the door, three maids are in uniform, scurrying from one part of the kitchen to another, preparing party trays and main courses. The smallest of the three women complains, "Does she really expect me to make biscuits from scratch? How crazy is that? If she wanted to serve biscuits with dinner she should've told us sooner so we could've bought some dough from the store! The nerve of that woman! What are we going to do?" she asks the other two.

"Well, I guess she's not getting them. We don't have time to go to the store now. Lisa, do you know how to make them?"

"No. I have nevah made a biscuit in my life. Do I sound Southern to you?"

Angela hesitates but opens the door completely and steps in. "Excuse me. I couldn't help but hearing your dilemma. I do happen to know how to make biscuits from scratch and I'd be happy to help if you'd like."

"Who are you?" asks Lisa, the largest of the bunch, as she puts the final herb garnishes on the backs of roasted quail lying in front of her on the kitchen island.

"I'm a guest who knows how to make biscuits," replies Angela, smiling kindly with both eyebrows raised. The three ladies look at her and shrug. "So? You want them or not?" Angela asks impatiently.

The three ladies look at each other in silent agreement as Lisa bends down and offers her a clean apron from the bottom drawer of the island in the kitchen.

"Thank you. My name is Angela. What's yours?" she asks, taking the apron and kicking her red heels off to the corner of the room.

"I'm Lisa. This is Sarah and Trudy."

"Nice to meet you all," says Angela, smiling warmly as she makes some room at the table. "I'll need some self-rising flour, Crisco, milk, and a preheated oven. Do you have those things?"

Gratefully, the maids get busy scurrying around the kitchen collecting the ingredients she needs. They watch intently as Angela takes off her rings, washes her hands, puts the apron over her head and demonstrates the art of southern biscuit making. "Of course, there are no real measurements. You put about two cups of flour in a bowl and cut the shortening into the flour," she says as she works shortening into the light and fluffy flour, each substance desperately clinging to her fingers as if resisting being mixed with the other. "Then you just add the milk until it feels right, until it's not sticky anymore. It's that simple, you just have to be gentle and it will all come together."

Sarah begins to speak while Angela gently kneads the dough, taking it out of the bowl and rolling it on the marble countertop of the kitchen island. "Mrs. Howard can be real demanding sometimes. She says she's been in love with the South all her life; swears she must have lived down here in another lifetime. But, all she really knows how to do is order us around and shop. She drives us crazy! We don't work for her all the time. We're just kind of on call. But, she'll have you to believe we live out back in a shack."

Angela shakes her head disapprovingly, folding one end of the dough over the other. "I haven't even had the pleasure of meeting her yet. But, I'll keep that in mind." Angela wonders where all the southern people in Atlanta have gone. She never sees them anymore. In most situations, she's the only native Atlantan. People are always shocked by this. It's as if they didn't really mean to invite her, a real Southerner, to their parties in their southern mansions, filled with southern heirlooms likely belonging to someone else's family. "The least they could do is learn how to make biscuits," she thinks to herself as she rolls the dough onto a sheet pan and begins cutting circles with a tin cup from the cupboard.

Angela finishes the biscuits, delicately lifting the cut out portions of dough from the table and placing them side-by-side on a baking sheet until it is filled. "Take them out when they start to turn golden brown on top," she advises, washing her hands and taking off the apron.

"You won't mention this to anyone will you?" Trudy asks, handing Angela her shoes.

"Who needs to know? And, it smells wonderful. I can't wait until dinner." Angela washes her hands, takes off her apron and replaces her heels. She slowly opens the small side door to the kitchen to make her way back to the hallway and foyer. To her surprise, Brent sees her come out of the doorway and enter the hall.

"Where have you been? I kept waiting for you to rescue me and you never came," he says as he wraps his arm around her shoulder and leads her to the living room where the party is now well underway.

"I was just looking around," Angela replies.

"You know you can't just look around people's houses uninvited!" he admonishes her whispering loudly.

"Well, I certainly do feel uninvited."

"I know. Dr. Howard was very rude to you in the foyer. I promise we'll leave here right after dinner. You won't have to spend more than that with these absolutely treacherous people."

The living room of the house is decorated in rich antique baroque style. Large mirrors encased in oversized gold frames line the walls just above the stiff, straight back sofa and chairs. Vases painted with plantation gardens and maidens adorn the top of every freestanding table without a purpose.

Brent leads Angela to a couple conversing next to a table filled with plates of American caviar atop cream cheese on wheat crackers. As they snack on the crackers, Brent motions toward Angela, his hand on her arm, and flashes his friendly smile.

"Janet, Tom, this is my wife Angela. She works downtown at the firm of Petrowski, Morgan and Kline."

"Oh, really?" asks Janet. "We have a next door neighbor that works there. His name is John Beckham. Brilliant attorney I hear."

Janet, a stay at home mother originally from California, keeps track of every resident in her new upscale neighborhood just minutes from downtown.

Angela, unable to say many good things about her coworker John, replies simply in a friendly tone. "Yes. John. I know him well . . . what a small world."

"So," interrupts Brent. "How long have you and Tom been in Atlanta?"

"Four years now." Tom replies. "I guess we are almost transplanted now. Isn't that what they say?"

"I think so," replies Angela, as she looks around him at the clock, wondering how much longer she will have to stay here.

"That's one hefty accent you have Angela. Are you from Tennessee?" asks Janet.

"No. I'm from here."

"Really? How nice" says Tom, surprised to actually meet someone from Atlanta.

"So." Brent interrupts. "Anyone know what's for dinner?"

Janet, already good friends with Mrs. Howard, the hostess Angela has not even met yet, informs with high pitched excitement. "We are having a southern feast tonight. Gail has been planning for weeks. Roasted quail with pine nuts, mashed potatoes and gravy, string beans, red cabbage and of course, biscuits. Do you like quail, Angela?"

"Sure," she says, even though she's not very fond of eating any meat still attached to a bone, much less in the shape of its original body. She thinks to herself "at least the biscuits will be southern."

All conversations are suddenly hushed when Mrs. Howard emerges from the dining room ringing a hand held bell. "Dinner is served," she announces gleefully. Everyone goes to the dining room to take their assigned seat at the enormous table that seats sixteen.

Angela enters the dining room behind Brent and can't help but stare in awe at the elegantly decorated table. All the plates, silverware and glasses match— white with pale pink roses inlaid in china with gold trimmings create an impressive scene. It all looks oddly familiar to Angela, who finds her name on a small card placed behind a place setting. As soon as everyone is seated, Angela's friends enter the room from another side door. Lisa, Trudy and Sarah carry plates filled with roasted quail. As they begin serving the main entrée, Dr. Howard begins to pass the side dishes, already prepared and waiting in their delicate serving bowls. Lisa, Trudy and Sarah return to the kitchen.

After everyone has prepared their plates, Lisa emerges with a basket full of piping hot biscuits. Angela's biscuits. Everyone takes one, impressed they are still hot, light and fluffy. "Oh my!" Janet exclaims from across the table, "Gail, you went all out! These look great!"

Mrs. Howard blushes a little, smiles and says, "oh it was nothing really. You'll have to thank my girls. They are so handy."

Lisa cringes at the comment, grips her basket firmly and doesn't say a word. Her thoughts remain appropriately trapped behind her lips, tightly pressed together in a fake smile as she rounds the table. Angela, offended for Lisa, quickly tries to lighten the air.

"I think the quail looks marvelous too . . . just perfect really. Not overcooked and just the right spices. I hear they are very difficult to cook just right."

Lisa acknowledges the compliment with a side-glance and a smile as she places the basket of remaining biscuits on the sideboard behind Dr. Howard.

"Thank you. What was your name again?" asks Mrs. Howard, realizing with slight embarrassment there is a guest at her table she has not greeted.

"Angela."

"Oh, yes dear. I remember now," she lies as she quickly shoves a fork full of mashed potatoes in her mouth.

The table conversations move effortlessly from one topic to another by the outspoken, gregarious guests seated at the table. Angela concentrates more on the food and thoughts of leaving than on the conversations. She can't help but think of other things while they discuss the finer points of Professor Howard's vacation home locations and which Four Star hotel has the best spa.

She can't help but think about how she is going to tell Brent she is taking some vacation time from work to go with Liz to Lexington in search of her dream family and husband. He would not be pleased. They had planned to return to England to visit his family sometime that year. If they were to do that, Angela would have to convince him that taking only two days from work would not jeopardize his trip. She quietly sits at the enormous table, smiling, laughing and shaking her head on cue, while she mentally calculates the arguments she will present to Brent after dinner on the way home. Cars are always the best way to promote communication. Short of leaving someone on the side of the road, you just can't escape. And Angela knows Brent would never do that.

After deciding her only option is to be open with Brent and tell him exactly how she feels, she relaxes and starts to enjoy her time at the table. Angela loves to sit back and listen to people. She can know more about a person just listening to their voices than they could ever tell her. Tiny details such as the way they hold their fork when they speak, the motion of their eyes, the way they tilt their heads, speak volumes to her.

After dinner, Angela spares no time reclaiming her husband, looping her arm in his and guiding him slowly in the direction of the ceramic magnolias calling out to her from the foyer. She can't stand to be around pretentious conversations for one more minute. If she has to stay, she's going to sneak back to the kitchen. Helping the maids clean would be less painful than hearing another minute of Dr. Howard's speech on his greatness. Brent, sensing her desperation as she loops her arm around his and gently tugs, gracefully apologizes and leaves the dinner party with Angela on his arm.

Once outside and in the car, Angela doesn't want to talk about the dinner party. Instead, she confesses right away. "Brent. I have decided to go to Lexington to do some research about these dreams. Liz has agreed to go along and help me."

"I knew you were going to do this eventually. I wish you wouldn't though."

"Why?"

"You know," he says cautiously as Angela's face, blank and irritated stares back at him demanding more explanation. "You have to be prepared that these dreams may not be true. You may get to Lexington and find things that directly contradict what you've been dreaming. It may not be about this family at all. You know you have to be prepared to accept that and just come home."

"I know that."

"Besides, there is very little chance that these dreams are real. You've already found some information about them that just doesn't add up." Brent parks the car on the side of the road in frustration.

"What doesn't add up?"

"You know! Okay. Let me spell it out for you. The house Liz found when she went didn't match the house in your dreams. You say it wasn't her house, but the cemetery says it was. You also say her husband had money and that he was a serious businessman. But, the census says he was a bartender and a grocery store clerk . . . Angela, he was just another guy with just another housewife. This guy didn't have money, didn't come from money, and their house wasn't the one you saw. You think you've confirmed the train connection she had with her family because everyone in her family was related to the railroad somehow. Everyone at the turn of the century had some connection to the railroad. That's not specific enough. All you have are some names, a time period and some dreams. Please don't go. You're just going to be disappointed."

"That's why I have to go. I have to know for sure. I am going. You don't have to believe. If you don't want me to share any of this with you I won't, just tell me now."

"That's not what I want. I want you to share. I just don't want you to be disappointed. It's so crazy!"

She looks out in the distance, takes a deep breath and slowly, quietly, calculating every word, responds, "Sometimes I think I am going crazy. The dreams are so real. But Brent, I'm there. I can see everything through her eyes. I hear with her ears. I can even *feel* her body. And smell. Have you ever smelled in a dream? The smells are just as real as the world around me tonight. I feel her pain, fear, laughter and love. It *is* real. And, as tacky as it sounds, it's beautiful." She looks away from him out of the car window and up at the full moon shining down on her.

Brent gently places his hand on her leg. "Angela. You know I will support you 100%, but you have to understand this is a lot for some people to take. They are going to attack you. They'll accuse you of all sorts of bad things—even call you a liar."

"I know. Most everyone I know here in the South will call me possessed—say this is all the devil's work. But how can something so beautiful be evil?"

Brent moves his hand away, tries to wipe the nervousness off his face and carefully chooses his words. "If you truly believe that what you are doing is right, then who are they to question? None of them have had dreams like this. None of them have been haunted every day by this family. None of them can understand. And, they don't have to know. This is your issue. Maybe if you go to Lexington they'll stop haunting us." He lowers his voice and grins while Angela continues to stare up at the full moon. "Besides," says Brent, "they already know you're a nut."

His humor doesn't even hit Angela's radar, but does manage to take her away from the grip of the full moon. Her eyes glisten in the moonlight and a small playful grin finds it way across her face. "It's all bullshit you know?" She says softly as she looks into his eyes. "The fear. The great religious paradox: Fear the unseen but have undying faith in the invisible. And all that time the proof is preprogrammed in our own dreams. It's a shame really, to take that away from so many faithful people. I'm not afraid of this anymore. I've never been so irrationally sure of something in my life."

"They'll never believe you," he says matter of factly.

"I know. I don't care. It isn't about religion, about proving reincarnation or disproving Christianity or rebelling against those Christian fundy freaks I grew up around . . . It isn't about them. It's about *me*. I need to know I'm not crazy! I need to know that it really is as real as it feels, even though it makes no sense.

In the end, if it's all true, then I'm the only one qualified to label it for myself. I cannot label the experience for anyone else. Frankly, I don't care what anybody else thinks. I'm just trying to rule out the need to admit myself to the nearest mental institution. And, I can promise you the jury is still not out on that. I've considered the possibility of a multiple personality disorder more than once, ya know?"

Brent laughs and starts up the car. "Will you ever stop litigating your life?" he asks as he looks at his wife with both admiration and disbelief.

Angela smiles. "I hope not. We should all pay so close attention." She leans over and kisses him on the cheek.

Extensions of Time

Liz's champagne colored Honda Civic races toward Kentucky along the mountainous highway just outside of Lexington. Angela is in the front passenger seat. "Only 20 more minutes," Liz announces.

"Good" Angela says, "I guess I should put on some makeup. I wouldn't want to scare anyone." She reaches into her purse, determined to find the mascara that has buried itself under mounds of small folded white papers the significance of which is long lost.

"There you are!" she says gleefully as she pulls out the mascara.

Angela reaches up to pull down the overhead visor mirror. She opens the mirror and becomes frozen in place. A large cobra, its head the width of the mirror, slowly uncurls itself and lowers its head to her face. Its small, round, black eyes stare deep into Angela's eyes. Its stare is so powerful Angela is positive it can see the very essence of her soul. The cobra is so close to her face she is afraid it will touch her nose. Her head presses back against the headrest, her breath becomes shallow, and she realizes the sound of her pounding heart is filling her body. The cobra notices it too and mercifully breaks its paralytic gaze into her soul.

It begins to lower its head, slowly following an imaginary road from the center of Angela's eyes down to her heart. As it descends, she cannot help but notice its long tubular body with lightly dusted brown scales glistening in the morning sun. She can't help but admire its beauty. Its movements are graceful and purposeful, its power undeniable.

The cobra stares into her heart, only inches away from her chest, with the same intensity it dedicated to her eyes. Slowly, it makes the journey north again back to her eyes. Its small round eyes now less threatening, Angela lets out a breath and whispers, "Thank you." She is not exactly sure why she is thanking this snake. Perhaps because it has not dealt her a fatal blow, perhaps because she understands it is about to leave. As if to say, "You're welcome", the cobra backs away, tail first into the mirror. Its head retreats, its eyes still level with hers until its image disappears altogether. The reflection of Angela's face is now visible in the visor mirror, her cosmetic touch-up long forgotten.

"Liz," says Angela in a slow, deliberate tone, looking at her friend. Liz is still singing along with the radio, oblivious to the large snake that had just descended from her visor. "Did you just see that cobra?" "Cobra?" Liz looks in her rear view mirror to see if she has run over anything. "What are you talking about?" she asks, sure that the mental breakdown she was expecting from her friend has arrived early.

"It was just here. He came out of your visor, checked me out and then went back into the mirror"

"What?!" Liz exclaims, realizing her friend is not joking. "Oh no! No cobras in my car. I'm pulling over right now!" She pulls over to the side of the road.

"I think it's okay though," Angela explains. "I think it's friendly. It didn't hurt me". She begs her friend to just leave it alone.

Liz screams in complete frustration. "Have you lost your mind? I'm not having a cobra riding with us in my car!" She gets out of the car and turns to slam the door, but something catches her eye. "Oh my God! I see it!" Liz can see part of the cobra's body winding itself in and out from under the seats in the back floorboard. She screams in terror and begins waving frantically to passing cars.

"Come on Liz," Angela begs, completely calm herself and irritated that her friend is not. "Let's go! Just leave it. It won't hurt us. You have to trust me!"

"We have to kill it!" remarks Liz, looking sternly at her friend.

"No!" Angela replies angrily "Don't kill it! Do not kill it!"

Angela is repeating these same words as she wakes up to the morning sun shining down upon her face.

"That is the wildest dream! It's so symbolic! The cobra coming from the mirror just as you start to better yourself by putting on makeup," Brent says as he drives towards the mall. In the months since their dinner party at the Howards', Brent has become more at peace with Angela's dreams. He understands how important they are to Angela and promises to support her regardless of the outcome of her trip to Kentucky, which he secretly prays will be a success.

"I guess so. But, why do I dream about the scary animals? Why can't I have symbolic bunnies or something like that?" jokes Angela.

"Why don't we look it up when we get to the mall? I'm sure the book store will have some of those dream dictionaries," Brent suggests.

"You can look it up if you want. I'm pooped. I just want to sit down with a good cookbook and relax."

Angela's dreams are exhausting her. She knows it probably does have significance, but she doesn't have the energy to research it at that moment. Food sounds like a great alternative. She doesn't like the dream dictionaries and dream doctors anyway. She thinks they're a waste of time. She laughs as she imagines what a dream doctor would say about her dreams. To try to interpret most of her dreams would be insulting and like admitting they aren't real. But she knows the cobra dream is not in the same class of dreams as the ones about Francine and Klairs. The cobra dream, although quite vivid, involved a present day situation and felt symbolic more than anything else.

Strangely enough, she knew the difference and maybe Brent was right, maybe a dream dictionary could tell her more.

Unfortunately, Brent is not going to let her go to the cookbooks right away. "Come on. We'll look this up and then go check out recipes later," he insists, pulling her hand in the direction of the New Age book section. "Okay," she replies, rolling her eyes.

They arrive at the most abandoned part of the bookstore, the New Age section. The New Age books are categorized by subject, and the dream dictionaries look like the only ones that have been touched since the store opened. They are the only books with crumpled jackets and less than one inch of dust on them.

Brent picks up a dictionary and starts to thumb through it. "Nothing here. Let me look at this one," he says as he takes a smaller book off the shelf. "Snakes! Here it is. Listen to this," he says as he points to the entry and reads aloud. "A snake is a phallic symbol used to represent your fears of sexual intimacy. If you feel threatened by a snake in your dream, it may be a terrible omen. Take precautions in the upcoming days." Brent looks over at Angela. Angela rolls her eyes. "Nope. That's not it. I've never been that scared of a penis. Total crap, put it back up." Angela starts to leave to go to the cookbook section when a book catches her attention. It is rather small but is misplaced, lying sideways on the bottom shelf, so she is able to spot it. "What is this?" she says, pulling the book from the corner of the bottom shelf. *"Shamanism: Animal Spirit Guides.* Here we go. Let's see what this has to say."

Angela shows Brent the paperback and flips to the index. There, she finds an enormous list of animals indexed. "Cobra. Look, they have it here! Not just snake . . . Page 43." She flips back to the correct page where there is a rather large picture of a cobra. The site of it creates a strange sensation in Angela's stomach. She reads out loud to Brent. "Shamans work with animal spirits as guides. Each animal possesses its own divine, innate powers and each teaches unique lessons. The Cobra's knowledge includes memory of the soul world, freedom from religious persecution and memory of past lives." Silence blankets them as they both process what they have heard.

Angela closes the book. "Well, I don't know about you, but I'm considering that one on point." She shakes her head in disbelief and looks back to make sure what she has just read is actually there. It is, and Brent is just as shocked. "Aren't you glad I insisted?" He smiles at her. "Yes, I am." She smiles back as she pats him on the back. "Now, let's go look at those cookbooks, if we can even think about food now."

Liz has spent the night with Angela so they can leave for Lexington early the next morning. Leaving Angela's house at 6:00 in the morning, they drive North through Atlanta on interstate 75, which will lead them directly into the city of Lexington, Kentucky.

The ride up I-75 is breathtaking. The highway leads them through many quaint mountain towns with breathtaking views. Angela starts counting waterfalls. They are small but easily visible next to the road. Angela and Liz laugh and talk about what a strange trip this is. "So, what if all this is real? What are you gonna do then?" asks Liz.

"I don't know . . . I guess I'll believe in reincarnation . . . I guess I won't be able to call myself a Christian anymore, not that that would be a tragedy I suppose."

"That's a tough one isn't it? Reincarnation is not entirely consistent with Christianity," Liz advises.

"Well, it's not that inconsistent if you just add it to the whole we live, die and go to heaven concept. You'd just be joining the two ends together. There's no problem admitting newborn babies come from heaven. There's no problem admitting that saved souls go to heaven. And, there's no problem admitting the impact of a soul's free will. So, why not? If a soul wants to come back again why couldn't they choose to? Is free will only for the living? If so, what is the purpose of heaven? Doesn't sound like any place I'd want to go to."

"True. But it throws the whole thing off balance. If you accept reincarnation, then what is the point in salvation, the basis of the Christian faith?"

"Maybe reincarnation is salvation. God is supposed to be just after all . . . why not give his children more than one chance?"

Silence falls between them for a moment as they consider each other's comments. Angela is prepared to consider the reality of reincarnation. Liz still skeptical, silently ponders enrolling in her church's apologetics courses to learn more about the scope of beliefs encompassed by her Catholic faith, and the history of reincarnation.

"Ya know," says Angela after about ten minutes of silence. "I have to really thank you for everything. It's not like I can talk to just anyone about this. Does this make us freaks? Because normal people don't usually do stuff like this, right?"

Liz laughs. "Well, if following your dreams makes us freaks, then so be it".

"Good answer!" says Angela, "You know, I don't really have a basis for understanding what's happening here. I've only been Southern Baptist all my life . . . well, until they kicked me out of the church and school. I guess they didn't think I was a good Baptist after all!" laughs Angela.

"What did they do to you?" Liz asks seriously.

Angela pauses for a moment and looks out her window at the crisp blue sky. Her tone grows serious as she chooses her words carefully. "They did what every cult and fundamentalist movement does to their children. They destroyed my faith in organized religion."

"How? How does that happen? I would think the opposite would happen."

"Yeah. They did too. But it doesn't. It starts out innocent enough. They tell you that in order to save yourself from hell you have to accept Jesus and not sin. No problem right? Wrong. They start teaching you what defines sin, and it turns out, everything is sinful. How you dress, the movies you like to watch, the music you listen to, the lust you feel for the hotty next door, your jealousy, your envy . . . the list goes on and on. Then one day, you realize that the very essence of who you are is sinful. And they perpetuate this realization in church by preaching that we're all born in sin."

"It creates a terrible turmoil deep inside and there's no escape. You have now officially sold your soul to a cycle of guilt. You have no choice but to hate yourself; to hate everything you are. I broke free of that. I don't hate myself anymore and I believe the very essence of my soul is something quite the opposite of sin; I think it's glorious. We are, after all, supposed to be made in God's likeness . . . Nobody was ever able to explain to me that contradiction in the Christian school or in church. They just yelled at me to shut up and stop engaging in blasphemy."

"Good God! Weren't you just thirteen?"

"I was thirteen when I got kicked out, but I had started asking questions long before then."

"You were just more than they could handle, Ang . Little kids don't normally think of things like that," Liz says as she smiles with pride imagining her precocious friend asking philosophical questions as a little girl.

They laugh together and Angela thinks to herself that she really is lucky to have such a great friend. Not only would Liz be discrete about the purpose of their trip, she would also be of great assistance for research. Law school had prepared them well for hours of grueling research in libraries and stuffy archives. She already knew they worked well together and that their research abilities complemented each other. She would have to rely on their basic research skills, first introduced in law school and later perfected by sheer necessity and fear of losing one's job.

All the pieces of her life were beginning to work together to a glorious finale. She knew every event was offering her the necessary pieces to prove the most important lesson anyone can ever learn in life, unconditional love. Her experience with the church early on caused her to reject all conventional religious beliefs and opened her mind to any possibility. Her education and training as an attorney gave her the means to set aside her emotions and objectively analyze her dreams. Her entire past now made sense. Luckily, she wasn't afraid of the truth they held and recognized the impact they could have on her life if they turned out to be real.

As they sit in silence, Angela goes over the list of research goals in her mind. She gets out her small notebook and begins to organize their research plan. She knows the library will be their greatest resource. Luckily, she has already inquired about the library hours and knows they will be open during the weekend and most nights. Because she will be there only half days for Friday and Monday, she needs to reserve their research time on those days for offices not open on weekends such as the courthouse and the church and/or cemetery offices.

Below every office on her list Angela notes why that office is relevant and with what dream it corresponds. Under the church, she notes the church dream, baptismal and birth records and the marriage. Under the cemetery she notes grave and lot locations, date of death and burial information. Under the courthouse, she notes the house dream, and marks the address from Gene's website, 207 Woodland Avenue. She also notes 315 West Maxwell Street, deeds, birth and death records, possibly even wills that had been registered through probate. She knows from law school that the best public records are always found in county court-houses. They hold property information, tax information, vital statistics and probated wills—documents that would bore most people but in this case are positively tantalizing.

Angela discusses the plans with Liz. "I was thinking we need to go to the courthouse first so we can find out when Klair bought their house on Woodland Avenue. In my house dream, they were already married, so it would be sometime after April of 1919. I also want to see if there are any other properties or information on them or their family members".

Liz agrees "Yeah, but how are we going to do all this in one half-day? You know title searches can take hours and we'd have to chase the titles all the way back to the early 1920s. And, let me remind you that we really don't know what we're doing. Neither of us has ever done a title search. All we can hope for is that the properties were owned by some old people who didn't move for a long time."

Angela's face fills with concern. "I know. But, maybe we'll find some other reference and we won't have to do an entire title search on the property. God, that would really suck. But, I'm confident we'll find whatever it is we need to find. And, if we don't, then big deal, we'll . . . well, I'll come back later."

Angela can't imagine the work that's before her and Liz at the courthouse. Liz was right. It could be an absolute nightmare, if they even find anything. Since they anticipate having the most difficulty at the court-house, they decide to go there first, mostly to assess the looming threat caused by the unknown. But, before beginning any research, they need to find the hotel, check in, and stretch their legs from the long ride.

Angela pulls out the map and directions and starts figuring out where I-75 is going to lead them into the city and which way would be the best for arriving at the hotel. Angela, new to the city, relies heavily on Liz's sense of direction and memory of the surrounding highways from her business trip months earlier. Although taking another highway called New Circle Road would be the most direct route for the hotel, Liz decides to take another route leading directly thru town. She knows from her previous trip that the city is small, and after six and a half hours of nothing but highway she's ready for a change in scenery.

They pull into Lexington, Kentucky around 1:30 in the afternoon with full intentions of going straight to the hotel just north of town. They head west down Main Street. Nothing looks particularly exciting about this city. The east side of town is small but modern. As they drive down Main Street, Angela looks out the window, warmed by the sun and partially blinded by its glare off the passing cars. She strains to see anything familiar, but finds nothing. Rows of beautiful houses are followed by quaint strip malls and restaurants. They approach the city and Angela feels a stirring in her stomach and excitement bubbling up into her chest. As soon as they reach the center of the city, known as Cheapside, Angela becomes completely alert and starts speaking very fast.

She points out the courthouse, but insists that Liz turn right onto a familiar street instead. "Where are you taking me?" demands Liz.

"I don't know. But I know this way. Just go there," Angela pleads, as she insists they take a left, then another left, then a right. With great excitement they find that Angela has taken them directly to the parking lot of St. Paul's Catholic Parish, the church of Francine and Klair's family. Liz is flabbergasted. Although the church is an enormous presence in the city of Lexington with its tall clock tower and beautiful exterior, it is not on the main street and not at all visible from the street where Angela had insisted they turn off. Angela has taken them directly to one of their main points of interest.

Angela giggles. "Well, I guess this is where we're supposed to start. Screw the hotel and courthouse! So much for my list!"

"I suppose so . . . look!" Liz gasps, pointing to a sign next to the parking lot where they have just pulled in. "You ask for a sign and you get one!"

Angela looks to her right and can't help but let out a nervous laugh at an actual sign, rather large in size, placed in the grass next to their parking space. In bright bold letters it reads, "ST. PAUL'S: REMEMBERING THE PAST . . . EMBRACING THE FUTURE." Chills run down their spines as they look at each other in complete and total surprise.

With that, they make their way from the back of the church to the front. The front doors are exactly as Angela dreamt, with two doors on either side of the church. Above them, there is a tall narrow window, consistent with the stained glass window with spades Angela had seen, but it appears to be plain with no colored glass. Angela goes directly to her door on the far right, only to discover it is locked. "Follow me. We'll just go in the back door," Angela says as she returns to the side of the church from which they've just come.

Angela walks confidently to a door they had passed previously. "Wait," says Liz, noticing there is another door farther back on the church's edifice. Angela ignores her, opening the door and going inside. To

Liz's surprise, this is the "back" door. It is the only back door available to the congregation and leads them directly beside the altar.

Once inside, Liz notices there are several people working on the electrical equipment and microphones, preparing for the upcoming Palm Sunday Mass. There are also two people vacuuming and cleaning. As Angela enters the building, she is struck by the beauty of eight tall, narrow stained glass windows situated alongside the pews, surrounding the congregation. Angela proceeds to the middle aisle, with Liz struggling to keep up with her as her pace is almost at a run. Angela races down the middle aisle toward the front of the church to see if the foyer is the one of her dreams. To her dismay, it is not as she dreamt it. It is almost unrecognizable to her. Liz just follows along, not recognizing anything familiar with regard to Angela's dream.

From the congregation, there are three doors leading to the foyer. Angela heads to the left door to proceed to the side of the church she would've entered from. She opens the door to a dimly lit, oppressive dark room. There is wood paneling on the wall, but it is cheap, made of a pressboard material rather than the real wood she had felt under her hand during the dream. She orients herself in relation to the front door of the church and takes a few steps as she had in her dream. At that point, she is nose to nose with a door. The door is closed and announces, "Men's Room."

A bathroom now occupies the most sacred place of her dreams. She cannot look up and see that beautiful stained glass. All she can look up to now is an exhaust fan to carry out the odors of dedicated Catholic men. She feels outrage and struggles to keep her voice low.

"Liz, can you believe this? They've put a bathroom right here in the foyer?!" She says angrily.

"Well, it is just a bathroom. People have to go somewhere." Liz can't believe her friend is so upset about a bathroom.

"Well," retorts Angela, "how would you like it if someone went to the foyer of your church, whipped it out, and starting pissing just before church?"

Liz is sure her friend has lost her mind. "Calm down. It is what it is. Do you see anything familiar?" she asks.

Angela thinks for a moment. Everything is familiar. She is positive this church is the one of her dreams. She tries to center herself and decides to let the bathroom outrage go for just a moment. Time constraints demand it. She places her left hand on the wall just outside the men's bathroom as she had in the vision, closes her eyes and lets Francine's memories flood her consciousness. As her eyes close, she can clearly see the layout of the church that is hidden by new walls, ceilings and electricity. The wall to her left transforms to the beautifully crafted square wood panels. Angela realizes the same carpentry work still adorns the doors and the bases of the tall slender columns inside the church.

The men's bathroom in front of her and the oppressive ceiling just feet above her head evaporate. Without the ceiling in the way, she can see in her mind that the upper choir loft is open to the center foyer and her favorite stained glass window visible from the congregation. At some point, they broke up the foyer by placing bathrooms between the middle and outer doors. The original wood paneling is only visible on two spiral staircases leading to the upstairs choir loft from the center door, on the doors and at the bases of columns inside the church.

With these memories comes sadness. Sadness that time has hidden the true beauty of the church. Time has precluded the current members from enjoying the beauty of a church that was Francine's and a community's for decades. Like aging flesh, time has robbed the church of its youthful, rich beauty. As they turn back toward the sanctuary, they are met by one of the cleaning staff.

"Do I know you?" she asks, looking toward Angela.

"No. I don't think so," Angela responds.

"Do you go to church here?" she asks, sensing something very unnatural about their interest in this place.

"No. We don't. Do you?" Angela responds.

"I don't either. It's just you looked very familiar. Did you grow up here?"

"No. This is my first time in Lexington." Angela smiles as she decides she should try to get information from the woman and settle her suspicions before she and Liz are both kicked out for trespassing.

"We're here doing genealogical research. We went to the front of the church to look for information regarding the church. Do you know where the registries are kept?"

"Oh yeah!" sighs the lady with a hint of relief. "You'll have to see Sister Frances out back. There's another little white building next to the parking lot. They may know what you're looking for"

"I'm sorry. Did you say Sister Frances?" asks Angela

"Yeah, Sister Frances. She should still be here."

"Thank you," responds Angela and Liz as they exchange glances of disbelief yet again.

As they walk out of the church towards the back parking lot, they laugh at the irony. Liz repeats the lady's words "Don't I know you from somewhere?" in humorous disbelief. "Well, maybe Sister *Frances* can help us out!" responds Angela.

She just couldn't believe the person that needed to help them find information about Francine and Klair could possibly be named "Frances." Angela suddenly feels like a pawn in a heavenly chess game being played by two angels laughing gleefully as they shoot down coincidence after coincidence, with each arrow hitting its mark.

Liz stops Angela from entering the small white building with Sister Frances' office right away. "Were those your stained glass windows?" she asks, eager to know if they have a validation.

"No. They were tall and narrow like the one I saw. But I didn't see it," she replies sadly.

"All of them have depictions of saints on them. Do you remember a picture, saint, or color of any kind?"

"No. I don't remember any religious drawings. It was very different. It had those spade thingies on it. Other than some blue, I don't remember a lot of color," Angela admits.

They reach the small white building the lady has pointed them to, and not surprisingly, are able to obtain all of the registries they are looking for in virtually no time at all. The secretary at the front desk, a short, kind woman, is eager to help them. She tells them the registries have all been returned from the dioceses only in the past week. Normally, they would be held there, but the diocese had sent them to the church. The church staff hadn't quite figured out what to do with them or where to keep them. So, for now, they are all tucked away in a filing cabinet.

The secretary invites Angela and Liz into a back office complete with desks, chairs, photocopy machine, computers, and phones. The girls that usually use this office space had both called in sick that morning. As a result, the secretary is able to offer them the desks in this space and invites them to make whatever copies they need. Angela and Liz start working immediately.

Angela's first interest is to find the marriage registry from April 1919, the month Francine and Klair were married. As she turns the old, partially yellowed but well preserved pages, she is amazed at the number of marriages chronicled on the pages. Every page she turns is a progression through time—1888, 1910, 1915 . . . Finally, she arrives at 1919 and searches for the month of April, scanning past unfamiliar names with her index finger.

She turns the page. The first entry contains the first written original document Angela has ever seen with both of their names—"Augustine Klair Weitzel" and "Francina Donovan." Their witnesses are noted as one "Margaret Donovan and Charles McCrystal". Angela is suddenly filled with nostalgia and a longing to experience her wedding. The book now open before her laid witness in the same manner at Francine and Klair's wedding. She runs her hand across the page and can envision the priest turning to the page before bending down to record their names on the new, crisp white pages.

Angela looks down at their names and turns back the page by one. "That's right. This is how it would be." She looks at the book filled with names to the bottom of the previous page. "These were witnesses," she thinks as she stares at the open pages. She imagines the priest recording the information after the ceremony, with her, her sister, and her husband's best man present.

The sound of a distant telephone ringing brings her back from the past and reminds her that the church's office will eventually close. Although she would love to stay there all afternoon and daydream, there is a lot of work still to do. She asks Liz to photocopy the entry and begins searching for Francine's baptismal record. She lifts the large registry book and locates the one corresponding to the year of her birth, 1895. This registry is filled with names and more difficult to search than the marriage records, which were organized with only approximately five marriages to a page.

The baptismal records certainly support the Catholic stereotype of large families. On each page there are approximately thirty entries. Luckily, Francine was born at the beginning of the year, so her entry is not far from the bold black elegantly handwritten header indicating the new year of "1895". About three fourths of the way down the page Angela locates her baptism. "Francina of Charles Donovan and Margaret Corrigan," baptized March 10, 1895. It is no wonder this church is such a large part of her memory. She was baptized here, grew up here, married here, and her death was surely mourned here as well. Angela could only wonder what it would feel like to have such religious consistency in her life.

Liz and Angela leave the church office with information on the time for Masses, thanks the staff and promise to return for Palm Sunday Mass. Angela suggests, "Let's try going to the courthouse again. We don't have much time before it closes, but maybe we can at least find the land records office so we don't waste any time on Monday morning before we leave."

"Great idea. We just have to find the courthouse."

"I know where it is. We don't need a map. We

passed it on the way in . . . at Cheapside. It's just up the road a couple of blocks."

"Okay. I'm going to trust your directions then," chuckles Liz.

They drive down the one-way street Angela has led them to and quickly arrive at Cheapside. An old, white marble building is surrounded by manicured green areas and looks like it should be the courthouse though few cars are around it. They easily find a parking space and walk to the front doors of the building. The building is deserted, and only signs indicating "moved to new building" hang on the doors. Liz notices a large bronze plaque hanging in the side courtyard that announces this building had in fact been the courthouse. Angela notices a construction worker hanging out at one of the entrances, so she asks him where the courthouse has moved to. "Well," he says in a gruff voice, "it used to be here, but now you can find it over there." He points down the street to a newly constructed, large grouping of buildings surrounded by another green courtyard. "Thank you," replies Angela as she races over to show Liz the new courthouse.

They walk to the new courthouse, which is actually two buildings joined together by a walkway and common courtyard. There are few signs, so Liz asks a group of security guards on a smoke break where she can find the county land records. They don't know but suggest they try another entrance in another building.

Liz and Angela walk to the other entrance where people are standing in line to go through metal detectors, and security guards are busy screening and directing visitors to the appropriate courtrooms and elevators. Liz approaches one of the guards and asks where they might find the land records office.

"What is that? Is that where you pay taxes?" the guard asks.

"You could pay taxes there. But it's where I would find information about land ownership. Or, where I would put a lien on your house, or do a title search on property," informs Liz.

"Oh yeah! I know what ya talkin' 'bout now. That's the County Clerk's office. It's over there behind the library. You know where the library is? It's about three or four blocks that way to the left. You can't miss it. There's a parking lot in between the two. But, it's gonna close in 'bout five minutes."

"Thank you. Do you know by chance what time it opens back up on Monday?" Angela asks, making sure to sound extra southern.

"8:00 sharp," the guard happily responds.

Liz and Angela thank the woman as they make their way back to the car. Now that they know they will not be spending Monday morning in the courthouse, but in a separate building called the County Clerk's office, they can plan better. They will not have to waste time on Monday morning trying to find everything.

Finally, they drive out of the city of Lexington to do what they had first planned to do—check into their hotel. There wasn't a need to return to the city until the next morning and Angela wants time to organize her lists, goals and write in her journal. They check into the hotel, take the keys to their room, unpack and get comfortable.

Located on the outskirts of town next to a highway, the hotel is filled with horse racing fans. Normally, the hotel caters to business travelers, as their early morning continental breakfast and business office for travelers suggests. But this weekend, rows of horse trailers and excited fans crowd the halls with their leather suitcases and cowboy hats.

Angela and Liz's room is perfect for their needs. There are two beds, a large clean bathroom and a large desk with a bright light perfect for Angela's notes. She takes over the desk, lining up her file folders and the accordion files, which usually accompany her to court filled with others' problems. Beside her file folders and notes she places her journal and a pen to record her most private thoughts.

Angela has mixed feelings already, and they haven't even completed a full day of research. On the one hand, she is happy to have found the church and feels a great familiarity and peace inside its sanctuary. Having escaped her oppressive religious childhood of independent Southern Baptist fanaticism, legalism and strict fundamental principles, she is not able to easily enter churches and feel peace. The day she was ostracized from the church and school, Angela vowed she would never again be a member of any church or congregation. Now, as a woman and wife almost twenty years later, she has kept her promise—until today.

This church feels so different. In Baptist churches, she is certain to experience anxiety, nausea, and a primal urge to run as fast as she can out the front door. She does not feel this at St. Paul's. She wants to sit in a pew and not move. She wishes there were nobody there that afternoon so she could have the church all to herself.

Angela feels bewildered by an unfamiliar nostalgia she previously believed was reserved only for the elderly. She feels centuries old and longs for a stained glass window she will never see again. From the outside of the church, it's clear there's still some sort of a window, but no colored glass is apparent and whatever window remains is covered by the ceiling that seals the church's true beauty.

Later that night, Angela sits at her hotel desk and writes in her diary. She describes how it once was, and how it is now. She writes about her regrets that the church "is now only a hull of what it previously was. It appears as though all is lost to time, ceilings, and the necessity of indoor plumbing."

Res Ipsa Loquitor:
The Thing Speaks for Itself

A child sings softly, swinging a teddy bear as her mother leads her to the children's book section of the library. "Row, row, row your boat, gently down the stream. Merrily, merrily, merrily, merrily, life is but a dream." The child turns to smile at Angela and Liz as they enter the Lexington Public Library.

The library lobby is dripping with elements of time. Its large round rotunda in the center of the lobby open to every floor contains an imposing pendulum hanging from the ceiling, swinging gently over a map on the floor. The swing appears to change direction on the map, just as time appears to pass. But, this is an optical allusion. The pendulum does not change its direction. The earth around it moves.

The pendulum swings over a beautifully decorated ornate map of the eastern United States. Most people hurry by the pendulum without much notice. For those curious enough to slow down and inspect the sight, a plaque and pamphlets detail its purpose.

Angela and Liz hurry by the pendulum without much notice at first. They have a mission to accomplish and give the pendulum only a passing glance to note the irony of its presence. Angela recognizes what it is immediately, as one use to hang in her local mall over a sand pit. She follows the pendulum to the ceiling, where a forty-foot ceiling clock looks down on her. It is the largest of its kind in the world. Time upside down.

She can't help but think this is all very strange. She has done her best to not eagerly search for "signs", but they keep appearing out of nowhere. Instead of giving this additional sign regarding time any more thought, she shakes her head in awe and makes her way with Liz to the elevator banks.

But what Angela and Liz don't know is that this library lobby dripping in time has something very in common with their visit to Lexington. The pendulum and clock were not always a done deal for the library. They were actually gifts from a very charitable philanthropist, Ms. Lucille Caudill Little, a ninety-one year old resident of Lexington. The Cincinnati Enquirer wrote about her generous gift on August 18, 2001 in an article entitled: *Idea came in a dream, philanthropist says.* Ms. Little admitted frankly "The idea came to me in a dream . . . I get some of my best ideas in dreams. They just hit me." The clock's installation was completed shortly before Liz and Angela's arrival.

Angela and Liz take the elevator to the fourth floor and follow the signs to the genealogy room. The room is small and separated from the rest of the library by large metal double doors. Inside the room, one wall is dedicated to microfiche, with large cabinets and two small tables with machines for viewing old reels of newspapers. The other wall contains rows of reference materials and books. A large cherry conference table commands the center of the room, surrounded by four chairs. Elsewhere in the room is a shadow box containing historical books on horse racing in Lexington and a small reception area with two leather wingback chairs.

Angela collects information by painstakingly surveying all the remnants of the past located in that library room. She searches each of the two newspapers circulated during Francine's life, reading every entry the week before, of and after her marriage. The facts on Angela's list become threaded together on her paper by small check marks. Every aspect of Francine's documented life begins to spring from the room, breathing life into her and her family once again.

Angela feels led to key points of information and is surprised to find her keen intuition lead her to facts peripheral to her own research. For example, Francine's brother Jerry made the news before he set out for World War I by getting into a fight with a Russian student, leaving the student blinded in one eye after his glasses shattered. Jerry, a local fireman at the time, defended himself by saying that the student had insulted a girl. The Jewish student league at the University was not impressed.

Angela also finds that Francine's nephew, little John Ramsey, thirteen years old when his aunt died, had grown up to become a priest. The entire family except Francine was there to witness his ordination with pride. He sang his first Mass at St. Paul's church in 1936.

Liz and Angela also find a variety of facts that validate Angela's list of facts from her dreams. One validation begins to follow another as Liz marvels at Angela's ability to concentrate and focus. For seven hours her focus does not waver, even during a quick lunch break. She finds one validation, prints out the evidence and moves right on to the next. Whenever Liz finds something, the same chain of events takes place. It's as if excitement, joy and the elation over being proved correct have been replaced by determination, urgency and conviction. Time is too valuable and their visit too short. There is no time for celebrations.

They leave the library that evening at closing time exhausted and unsure of how much they've accomplished. Angela's folder is filled with copies of old newspaper articles, census reports and school rosters— pieces of time stuffed in a folder under Angela's arm. "Can you take me to the cemetery now?" Angela asks Liz, who already knows the way from her last business trip. "Sure," she replies.

Calvary Cemetery, the small Catholic cemetery of Lexington is located directly across from Lexington Cemetery, where most of Lexington's Protestants were buried. Gated by large iron fences and stone columns, Calvary cemetery is dotted with large trees and headstones from centuries past. Liz drives under the tree branches, slowly approaching the Donovan family plot, not far from the main entrance of the cemetery. She parks the car, gets out and leads Angela to the same headstones she has already met.

Angela feels no emotion, no connection to these stones with writing on them. "They are the only tangible reminders these people existed," she thinks to herself. She wonders how many times the people in these graves mourned for one another, only to join them later by their sides. There are no other mourners at the cemetery that day. Old cemeteries have few visitors to mourn for their dead. But, you aren't officially dead until you are forgotten. And, as Angela looks down at Klair and Francine's grave, she muses to herself that they are the only ones at the cemetery still alive, because she remembers them.

Liz and Angela don't stay long, as both are eager to return to the hotel room to regroup for the next day.

They are truly exhausted and happy to see the sun beginning to set through the trees and behind the headstones. Tomorrow would be more relaxed. They would go to an early Sunday Mass and visit the park, which according to the map, was located next to 207 Woodland Avenue, the house Gene's website reported as the residence in 1920. It would be an easy day, or so Liz thought.

That night, Angela begins to organize her articles and the lists from her dreams. The papers strewn across the hotel bed begin to paint a picture and fill in gaps she was not privy to from the dreams alone. She is finally able to relax as a calm surrender envelopes the room. Angela sips a glass of red wine as she looks at the articles, reading portions from time to time to Liz, seated on her hotel bed reading a novel, also enjoying wine.

Angela's favorite articles have to do with Francine's wedding. Angela located these articles by painstakingly reviewing every newspaper printed in Lexington the week of, before and after her wedding. It helped that the calendar days for 1919 were exactly the same as the present year, 2003.

Francine and Klair were married at 8:00 in the morning at St. Paul's on Tuesday, April 22, 1919. The bride and groom each had only one attendant. Francine was accompanied by her sister, Margaret. Klair was attended by his best friend, Charles McCrystal from Chicago.

The evening before the wedding, a rehearsal dinner was held at Francine's mother's house on Curry Avenue. Klair's friend, Charles McCrystal was there, along with Francine's large family. Some of her older, already married sisters and their husbands came from out of town to attend the festivities. They had established their families in the neighboring towns of Ludlow and Georgetown.

The early ceremony was attended by a large crowd, despite its being scheduled on an early Tuesday morning. The air was crisp as the guests arrived with their gifts to a beautifully decorated church. The inside of the church was conservatively decorated in spring flowers and palm fronds while Easter lilies overflowed from the alter. Francine wore a blue tailored traveling suit and carried a bouquet of small pink roses. Her sister Margaret was similarly dressed, in blue, carrying roses, wearing a matching hat.

Angela feels pulled to the past by words written almost a century ago. She can clearly imagine herself walking down the aisle of St. Paul's, her figure silhouetted by the hazy morning glow of the front stained glass window, open to the congregation, guiding her forward to her groom.

Reality returns her to her senses and Angela feels silly thinking of such things. But the image does help to remind her of a similar, more familiar event that took place only eight years ago—her own wedding. She went against southern tradition and insisted on keeping everything simple. She also had only on attendant, her bridesmaid. She wore blue and they both carried lilies down the aisle.

Angela takes another sip of wine, letting it slide down her throat, warming her stomach. She turns to the next set of articles and grins, with pride. Klair did in fact come from a prominent family. By far the most prominent was his uncle, William F. Klair, "Billy". Although he owned numerous businesses at different times in his life, he was most well known as a politician.

Author James Bolin, in his book *Bossism and Reform in a Southern City*, dubs him the "undisputed czar of Lexington, Kentucky for decades."

He was a part of the Democratic political scene for fifty years, dominating the party during most of that time. Uncle Billy grew up in Lexington, went to school and church at St. Paul's, and was elected as a page in the Kentucky House of Representatives at just fifteen years of age. He quickly advanced to messenger, the Speaker's page, and finally Assistant Sergeant-at-Arms in the Senate. By 1900, he was a representative for Lexington in the state House of Representatives, a position he held undefeated for six terms. Prior to his death, in October of 1937, he was Postmaster General. Photos in the newspaper send chills down Angela's spine. The resemblance between Billy Klair and the man on her train is striking.

Klair's father Jerome, married two of Billy Klair's sisters. His first wife, Agatha, Klair's mother, died when he was only a child. His father quickly remarried Agatha's sister "Lizzy" and had another child. Klair's father was also a bartender and apparently well known in the community. His death was announced on the front page of the *Lexington Herald* in June of 1917.

Klair's Uncle "Hense", was an expert betting commissioner in the county and reportedly known by every prominent horseman in the United States and Canada at the time of his death. Another of Klair's Uncles, Patrick Mooney, was a long time associate of Billy Klair. He was also involved in politics, serving on many county committee boards ranging from Accounting to Parks, to the Railroad Committee. Unfortunately, in 1911 he was murdered. His murder was reported on the front page of every newspaper in Lexington. The newspapers reported there was a dead body, several eye witnesses, a smoking gun found ditched in a nearby yard, and a confession from Thomas Dolan, a local attorney. Patrick Mooney was also Uncle Billy's business associate.

But despite Billy Klair's alleged reputation in underhanded politics and domination in Lexington, Thomas Dolan could not be found guilty of Mooney's murder. He was acquitted two years to the day of his arrest, five juries later. The murder took place in the Leland hotel, a hotel owned by both of Klair's uncles, Patrick Mooney and Billy Klair.

The Leland Hotel was touted as the finest of its time, with a full service bar and restaurant and over one hundred rooms with fantastic new renovations. Billy Klair sold the hotel after the murder. Angela's childhood dream was confirmed, but not easily. This validation almost slipped through Liz and Angela's hands, as the library incorrectly indexed the hotel articles under "W.T. Klair" instead of "W. F." or "William F. Klair". Liz was shocked to find what Angela insisted was really there.

Klair also had a prominent aunt described by most accounts as a quintessential socialite. Her name was Mary Slavin. She married Billy Klair in 1900, but never had any children. Her death also made the front page of the newspaper, even though she died seven and a half years after her well known husband. Even at the age of 72, she continued to be active in the community, on several church boards at St. Paul's and serving on various charitable committees. Together, the couple was well known for their philanthropy. Money was never an issue at the Klairs' estate, located just one block from the street named after them.

Francine did marry well. Angela was right. The census only told a fraction of truth. Everything subjective from the honeymoon train dream was confirmed. A writer for the *Lexington Herald* called Klair "a prosperous young business man of the city". He was thirty-two, and arguably from the most well-known family in Lexington at that time. Francine was twenty-four, and from a family that rarely made the papers. Angela was also correct about their ages from the honeymoon train dream.

The earth seems boundless as Angela revisits and allows the miraculous validations to flow over her. The family connections, the aunt, the resemblance of Billy Klair to her Klair from the train, all leave Angela in a state of wonderment. Francine is always with her.

Angela takes the last sip of her wine, places the bottle on the nightstand, reaches on the floor for her journal and begins to write.

I'm not sure when I first met Francine. I only know that her thoughts and memories accompanied me at a very early age, making my dreams as sweet as any mother could ever wish for her child.

Palm Sunday: Messages of Rebirth and Resurrection

The warm, still night air drifts into Angela and Liz's hotel room through a partially opened window. Angela is sleeping soundly, unmoved by the noises from a party down the hall, thrown by horse racing fans. Slowly, lightly, Angela's dreams slip into the past.

She once again finds herself in Francine's life as she begins making her way up the same staircase she ascended previously with Klair. Suddenly, she is pulled back by Klair as he wraps his arms around her waist and swings her to the floor. "Come on!" he giggles childishly, "I have something to show you!" Grabbing her hand, Klair leads Francine through the front hallway of the house to the back door. "What are you up to?" she asks.

Klair leads Francine out the back door and into the yard where she sees her prize immediately. In the back right corner of their yard, Klair has placed a potted rose bush overflowing with small pink buds. Francine places her hand over her mouth, squeals with delight and gasps "Oh! Thank you so much. They are beautiful!"

Klair passes his hand down her cheek to her chin, draws her into his chest and whispers quietly, slowly, "This is so you'll always have roses from me . . . so you'll never forget how much I love you." Francine smiles, her body filling with the warmth of his love.

Her eyes close, savoring the beauty of the moment. A tear of joy escapes and rolls down Francine's cheek.

Francine's tear remains on Angela's face as she awakens to a still, dark hotel room in the predawn hours. With her body wrapped in a beautiful sea of poetry, her mind struggling to maintain the imprints of his embrace, Angela can endure no more. Her body begs for his warmth. She wants desperately to reach out to him, to remain a part of his life. But she knows he is gone— his body crushed by sands of time. Angela is left only with the constant apparition of his soul to haunt her.

Angela and Liz awake the next morning exhausted. They have not stopped the entire weekend, but are committed to going to Mass that morning. Liz is a bit confused by her friend's insistence that they attend Mass. She knows that normally Angela would not behave like this. She usually couldn't be dragged into a church, much less insist that they go. Nevertheless, Liz is excited not to miss the opportunity to attend Mass in such a beautiful church. She suspects Angela's insistence on attending is only an excuse to spend more time inside her own sanctuary.

They leave in plenty of time to get to the church. Angela packs her camera and checks to make sure she has everything else she could possibly need such as extra batteries, her purse, tissues and sunglasses. They leave the hotel and head south toward town. Liz and Angela ride along in silence—the byproduct of exhaustion. The Mass will be a welcome respite, a chance to sit in one place for an extended time period without having to think much or concentrate on looking for anything. Angela will take this opportunity to take pictures that she wasn't able to take the day they arrived. This will be her second and last time at the church, at least on this visit.

Liz drives while Angela obsessively checks her camera equipment. The church is only a ten-minute drive from their hotel, and the car seems to drive itself at this point since they have traveled the same road countless times over the past two days. Angela looks up and out the window at the modest houses and cars lining the street's sidewalks. Across from and just north of the houses is a mental institution. Angela thinks how funny it is that she had to pass a mental institution every day she goes in to town for research. Surely that is some sort of cosmic joke! As they pass the mental institution, her attention is drawn back to the cars parked on the side of the street. Coming up on her right is a large brown 1974 El Camino with dark tinted windows. In bright white silhouette on the back window is a large image of a cobra.

"Slow down Liz! There's a cobra!" she manages to yell as they pass by.

"What?" asks Liz, not sure if she should back up to drop off her friend at the mental institution.

"Right there! We just passed it! A car with a huge cobra on it! And the car wasn't even a mustang! That cobra had no business being on that kind of car!"

"Oh. That's all . . . well, I suppose that's a good sign," she chuckles. Liz is on symbolism overload by this point.

"I suppose the cobra is glad we're going to Mass," Angela responds, amused at yet one more unexpected sign.

"Or pissed," Liz suggests.

Angela takes this sighting as a positive sign—sign that again, she is not alone in this journey. She closes her eyes and says a quick prayer to whomever might be listening. Angela thanks them for all the wonderful validations she has received already, promises not to continue to be upset about the church bathrooms, and honestly declares she is satisfied with all she has been given on the trip.

When they park in front of the church, it is still quite early and very few people have arrived. Angela gets out of the car and starts taking pictures of the exterior of the church, while Liz gathers her things and begins making her way up the stairs to the entrance. Only the front middle door is open, which disappoints Angela who has dreams of entering the door to the right just as she had done in her dream. She does not complain however, and follows her friend Liz into the sanctuary, feeling safe and secure behind her Catholic friend. Maybe no one will notice she isn't Catholic.

"Where should we sit?" asks Liz as she begins walking past the sparsely occupied pews. "You decide," Angela replies, remembering that the seat would only be temporary as Liz had briefed her the night before that for Palm Sunday you start outside so that the entire congregation enters together, carrying palms.

Liz picks a pew and they quietly sit down, once again awed by the high ceilings and tall narrow stained glass depictions of saints. They both feel humbled. Liz grins, silently pondering the significance of being surrounded by these blessed individuals who experienced heavenly miracles and visions during their lifetimes. Angela takes out her camera and discreetly begins taking pictures of the interior stained glass windows when a woman behind her taps her on the shoulder. "Excuse me ma'am, but, you can get a better picture from the loft upstairs. Would you like me to take you there?" she offers.

"Thank you! Why that would be great. I know where it is. I just didn't know if I could go up there," Angela responds.

"You can if it's open. But, I have the keys if it's locked. Follow me. I insist."

The door is not locked so they make their way up the stairs. "Is this wood original to the church?" asks Angela, as her hand runs along the wooden handrail while she climbs the stairs.

"Yes. It is. It's in pretty good shape too."

"I see that."

"Here we are. This is the choir loft. As you can see, there's a much better view of the stained glass windows up here. You can also see the organ, which has been here for a long time."

"It's all so beautiful." And, without thinking Angela blurts out, "What happened to the stained glass window in the front of the church?"

"Oh! That is my favorite window. Remnants of it still remain. Would you like to see it? I can see if the door is locked."

"Can we? I would really like that."

"Sure we can. I'm on the church's preservation committee, so I have access to it," the lady says as she struggles to open a small door at the back of the choir loft. It finally gives way, releasing a musty odor from its interior. "Excuse the dust! We don't come up here often," she says, stepping inside, happily leading Angela where few members have ever stepped foot.

Inside the door, a dark hallway leads to another door, which has a lock. The woman plays with the lock, opening it and the door it protects. Behind that door is a small wooden staircase. Angela follows her up the stairs. "Be careful where you step," she warns. "These steps are so old it can get dangerous . . . you never know." Angela heeds the warning and fights the urge to knock her guide over, run past her, and get to the window. At the top of the stairs, she can see a warm glowing light begging her to discover the origin of its brilliance. She reaches the top of the stairs, turns to her left and stands in awe.

Finally, in front of her, is *her* stained glass window. It is exactly as she remembers it. An audible sigh of relief escapes her lungs as she stares at the beauty before her.

A strange sense of entitlement, superiority and nostalgia run through her veins, praising and cursing the boards below her feet—boards that seal the image from all but simultaneously elevate her to stand before its sacred presence. Like the truth of her memories, shining bright in complete darkness, locked away from believers and hidden from their worship rituals, its truth is relegated to obscurity.

Angela can hold back no longer. "This was all open before. There were no bathrooms in the foyer. No ceiling. You could see this window from the foyer and the open doors below. The choir loft hung over the corners of the foyer, open in the middle and framed by this window. The organ was there too, at the base of the window. And the wood . . . the paneling on the walls matched the wood paneling on the staircases to the choir loft and the base of the columns. Why did they take it down?"

"I . . . I don't know. That was all before my time. This has been like this since the 50s I think."

Angela looks back at the window. "It's so beautiful. Did you know you could see this window from the congregation inside the sanctuary?" asks Angela, no longer censoring the words leaving her mouth.

"Yes. You're right. Turn around."

As Angela turns from the window, her eyes adjusting to the darkness, she sees an old wooden staircase leading to a dark space above her head. Behind the staircase is a concrete arch, its view sealed from the congregation below with wooden boards and iron rails. The arch, sad but proud, stands stoically in front of the stained glass window like a glorious frame whose picture has long been covered.

"Thank you so much for taking the time to show me all of this. You have a wonderful piece of architecture here and you should be very proud. Do your best to take care of it," Angela says while snapping some pictures of her window.

"Don't worry! I will. I love this church," she says, smiling genuinely, leading the way back down the narrow, dark, creaking staircase. Angela takes a few more pictures of the sanctuary from the loft and then makes her way, with her guide, to the pews below. She takes her seat next to Liz and whispers, "It's there. My window. Just like I said. It's there. It's all true. No more doubts." She quickly shows Liz the window on the viewing panel of her digital camera. Liz, squinting to see the details, smiles and whispers, "Your spades are called fleurs de lis."

Angela follows Liz blindly through the service that day. She stands like an iron maiden outside in the courtyard grasping a dead crunchy palm given to her by a little boy in a white robe. She hears faint voices coming from a microphone and then follows a group of people back inside the sanctuary to reclaim their seats. Messages of rebirth and resurrection resound from the biblical gospels as they are collectively read out loud by the parishioners. Angela stands frozen in place.

Every word pierces her wounded soul, sending waves of healing pleasure and pain throughout her body and out through her tears. She can't help but laugh in between her tears. Who else could appreciate the irony of her greatest validation occurring in a church? A stained glass window in a Catholic church would be one of the many reasons she would leave Lexington tomorrow believing wholeheartedly in reincarnation. "God and his crew must be laughing his ass off at me" she concludes mentally with a smile. "Thank you! I get it! I get it!" is all she can think of in response.

Angela and Liz return to the hotel room with a mixture of relief and happiness. The church at St. Paul's had been so welcoming. Neither felt like a stranger. Angela felt as if she belonged there and regretted she could not return every Sunday to sit inside her church.

They change clothes, pull out the map and plot their next move for after lunch. Liz pours over the map, locating Woodland Avenue. To her surprise, it is next to a park, Woodland Park.

"So you think this Woodland Park is your park? It's right next to Woodland Avenue, where Gene's information said she lived?" Liz asks.

"We won't know until we get there. But, it makes sense. Let's go!"

Angela loves the drive into the city of Lexington. The roads are sheltered by rows of trees with elegant Victorian houses peeking from behind. Liz turns onto West Maxwell Street and follows it straight until she arrives at 315 West Maxwell. Liz pulls the car into a small parking lot in front of the house and announces to Angela.

"There's the *Shambala Meditation Center.* Do you want to take a picture?"

"Yeah. I do. Thanks." Angela steps out of the car and laughs again. She cannot believe that this house is now a meditation center. The irony borders on campy. The house is familiar to her but is not the house she saw in her dreams. Perhaps she lived here at some point, or it belonged to someone else in the family.

They continue down West Maxwell, which soon becomes East Maxwell. Angela begins to shift in her seat, eager to examine every house, corner and tree they pass. "Slow down," she begs Liz. "Let me look." In no time, they are at a park. Liz slows down and pulls over to the side of the road to parallel park between two older cars parked on the side of the street.

"This is amazing," says Liz. "It's exactly like you said! Who would know there was even a park here? Do you want to get out?"

To her surprise, Angela answers, "No. This is the park, but I wasn't sitting here with Greta. I was over there facing High Street. Those are the houses I saw," she says, pointing to a street running perpendicular to the street Liz has parked on. The houses are beautiful in a quaint Victorian style, with crafted woodwork on the porches and gabled roofs. "And in that large hole over there to the right, there used to be a pond."

"You don't want to get out?" Liz asks again, perplexed by her friend's calm manner and resistance to sit in her park.

"No. Let's go to Woodland Avenue and see this house Gene's info says she lived in. We don't have time to sit around in a park. We can come back." Woodland Avenue is less than a block away. The narrow street is lined on one side with a block of quaint one- and two-story shops. Liz quickly finds the number 207 and proudly announces to Angela they have arrived. But, Angela appears confused and disappointed. Worried by her demeanor, Liz asks her friend, "Are you okay?"

"I'm fine. This block hasn't changed, it was shops

back then, just as it is now. I remember it!" Angela declares in stoic wonderment.

"But didn't the website say this was the address on her daughter's birth certificate in 1920? I'm sure these buildings are new, or there were probably houses or apartments or something here back then."

"No. This was all here but she didn't live here." Angela feels a recognition for everything around her. It all feels familiar and unchanged.

"So what now?" asks Liz, frustrated by her friend's stubbornness. "It matches! It's close to the park like you said," she insists, eager to claim yet another validation for her friend.

"Yes. But it's too close . . . Can you stay parked here? My feet need to touch this ground." Angela speaks as if in a trance. Liz senses that if she were to speak again, Angela would not hear her. She remains quiet and does as her friend has asked. Angela gets out of the car and proceeds to turn around slowly in circles. Liz is sure she has lost her mind.

Finally, Angela appears to orient herself to this place she has never been in her current life. She walks to the corner of Woodland Avenue and East Maxwell Street. She looks at the park on her left less than one block away. She looks at a brick fire station across from her. "That fire station was here too," she says confidently to herself as she crosses the street and begins walking alone away from the park.

Angela closely examines every house she passes. She asks herself, is the door in the middle of the house? Does it have a large upper right window? Does it have a big tree out front or is it close to the street? None of the houses fits her description, and after six blocks she turns around feeling defeated. She only looks on one side of the street. She knows she did not live on the other side of the street. She turns around to head back to the park, back to Liz and the car.

Suddenly, the April winds shift as the sun begins rapidly fading to gray and droplets of snow fall from the sky. A chill runs through Angela as her body is filled with the wintry air. She places her hands inside the pockets of her new wool coat. The soft stride of her tennis shoes becomes the firm steps of winter boots, avoiding snow and ice strewn across the sidewalk. Her breath fogs her vision as she passes a fire station and follows the street's slight curve to the right. The park is now on her left. She turns to face the park, noticing a group of children playing baseball as she begins to cross the street. "How nice the boys are letting her play," she says under her breath as she watches a girl up to bat, her dress hanging below her coat, with boots poised and ready to run as the bat lies confidently on her tiny shoulder. A pain streaks through Angela's side as the clouds, snow, cold air and winter wool coat disappear.

Once again, Angela can feel jeans hugging her legs, resisting her every step as a slight spring breeze flows over her bare arms in a sleeveless spring sweater. Her feet move freely in her tennis shoes as her lungs breath in the warm April air of 2003.

"The kids played ball where the adults now play tennis. I lived on this street . . . on this side of the street. I passed the fire station every day I went to the park." She runs back to the car and repeats the same sentences to Liz, still waiting for her inside the car.

"So she lived on the south side of East Maxwell Street?" Liz confirms.

"Yes. I'm positive. That is the way she walked to the park every day!"

"Okay. Whatever you say. Do you want to go back to the park for some more pictures?"

"Yes. But we have to make it quick. We have to go back to the library."

"The library? Why?"

"I have to find something that proves Gene's information about their residence at 207 Woodland is wrong."

"How are you going to prove him wrong when he obviously has something that says they lived at that address? Ang , we were there seven hours yesterday!" Angela turns away from Liz completely even though she continues to speak. Liz pleads with Angela. "Do you not remember? Oh, please don't make me go back. They're going to close about an hour from now anyway."

"You don't have to go if you don't want to. Just drop me off and I'll call you on your cell phone when I'm ready."

"All right. We'll go!" says Liz, taking a deep breath and starting her car to the library once again.

The parking lot of the library is nearly deserted when Liz's car pulls in. On this beautiful spring Sunday in the late afternoon, most Lexingtonians are tucked away in their century-old houses preparing meals, or are outdoors playing with their kids or planting their spring gardens. They aren't thinking of the families that lived in their houses one hundred years ago. They aren't thinking of the endless cycles of love, happiness and death witnessed by the wise eyes of their homes. They don't know they are no different from the people who lived one hundred years before or that their emotions are the same.

There is a different person working in the Kentucky genealogy room that day. She sits weary eyed checking her watch every ten minutes, sure that half an hour has passed. Disappointed, she continually returns to her business of sorting cards. Angela doesn't know what to look for or how to find proof that the addresses on Woodland Avenue contained businesses, not homes. She decides to go with what she knows, newspaper reels.

For the first time since arriving in Lexington, Angela actively begins thinking of Francine's death. She has had no dreams of it but is sure there is an obituary somewhere. Angela pulls out the microfiche reels containing February 1923 newspapers, feeds them to the machine, and begins searching. She reviews the ads in the newspapers for mention of businesses on Woodland Avenue. She reviews each day's death notices. Surely if there were businesses on that street, they would think to advertise in the newspapers? Surely if Francine's death was published, she could find it this way too? To her disappointment, she finds nothing as time begins to accelerate, much to the library worker's glee.

Liz, who reluctantly has joined Angela again in the library, decides to take a quick rest in the large leather chairs in the small room. Her head back, body relaxed, she falls fast asleep to the sounds of the microfiche reels advancing through time as Angela looks intently for clues to her remembered past.

Finally, the triumphant library worker's watch hits a quarter to five, fifteen minutes until closing. A voice from the central intercom announces the library will close soon. Angela sits back feeling completely defeated and frustrated with the uncooperative advertisers as Liz lets out a loud snore. They both laugh as Liz looks over to Angela and whispers "Was that out loud?" Angela nods, and grinning at her friend says, "It's okay. We can go now. The library is going to close now anyway."

"No. That's okay. We may as well close it down. Go ahead and finish whatever you're doing."

Angela turns around and continues advancing time through a microfiche machine while Liz rises from the chair, stretches, and begins looking through the shelves full of old books, studies and demographic research. She reads along the titles, her head tilted to the right, amazed that anyone cared enough to write or even read about most of the titles. Her eyes, glazed by the faded Dewey decimal symbols, stop on a row containing two books entitled simply "Directory". One is dated 1917, another 1923. "Could it really be that simple? Are these phone books?" Liz wonders as she pulls them off the shelf and begins flipping through the pages.

It's a phone book! "Angela! Come here! Come here! I found a directory, like a phone book! Look! 1917 and 1923." Angela drops everything and rushes to her side.

"1923? That's the year she died! What does it say?"

"It's organized by streets. Let me find Woodland Avenue. . . . Well look at that. Angela strikes yet again!"

Liz turns the pages until she reaches Woodland Avenue. The entry for 207 Woodland Avenue in 1923 contains "The American Shoe Hospital" in 1923. It was in between Paren's Dairy Products and Woodland drug store. On the corner, sat the Piggly Wiggly grocery store. Across the street sat the brick fire station Number 5.

Angela hugs Liz tight, takes the book, and runs to a copier. Liz immediately runs to another photocopy machine and begins making copies. The library worker jingles her keys, annoyed that Angela and Liz are threatening her decision to close the doors to the genealogy room three and a half minutes prior to the magical hour of 5:00. The photocopy machines light up, cooperate, and spit out copies of Angela's evidence as fast as she and Liz can insert coins.

Once back in the car, Angela begins to look closely at the few photocopies they managed to make. She is so grateful to Liz for giving her a second chance, not only to go to the library, but to confirm her suspicions about Woodland Avenue, based solely on a "feeling". Angela is amazed by the effort that went into a city directory at the turn of the last century. She is sure genealogists around the world are slowly going needlessly blind trying to read census reports when all they really need is a city directory. But who would think to look up their family of yesterday in the same form we look them up today?

The 1917 Lexington City Directory is alphabetized by surnames. Entire families, even their children, can be found by locating their surnames. In 1917, Francine lived with her family at 410 Curry Avenue. There were nine in the house, just two years prior to Francine's marriage to Klair. Out of all her sisters, Francine was the only professional woman in the house. She was a trained nurse. Her brothers were all engineers for the railroad, while her sisters worked in clerical positions and her younger sister Elizabeth and brother Charles attended school. Angela shows this to Liz, then turns to view 1923 again.

The 1923 directory is categorized by street names. Each person is found according to the street they lived on or who their neighbor was. As Angela flips through the photocopies, she notices that in haste she has copied the list for West Maxwell Street. Three hundred fifteen West Maxwell Street, the house Liz had toured because the cemetery records said it was Francine's last known address, was actually Francine's mother's address the year she died. Francine never lived there. Now, Angela is making validations in reverse, her instincts proving documented evidence wrong, more than once.

They are barely out of the library driveway when Angela makes another request of Liz, still high from the directory find. "Can we try to find this Curry Avenue? I think it may be where I had that potato dream. That is where I would cook with my sisters."

"Is it on the map?"

"Yeah, it's right here . . . a little south of town . . . close to the horse stables."

The night air is taking over as the sun begins to sink behind the horizon. They make their way towards Curry Avenue, missing streets and running stop signs as Angela tries to make sense of the map. Finally, they find their road and turn with great anticipation. The street is filled with houses, closely built, one story, with small white porches. "What are we looking for again?"

"We're looking for 410 Curry Avenue . . . or little half windows on the side of the house. That's where I looked out from the kitchen, tiny little windows. It should have a cellar in the back too," says Angela as she strains through twilight's haze to read the numbers on the homes. The homes are now surrounded by industrial development, a small historical enclave on the verge of a hostile industrial takeover.

They drive through without finding the number 410. At the end of the street, Liz turns the car around. The last house on Curry street facing south shows Liz and Angela its side. Towards the back of the house are two half windows.

"I bet you my first born that's the kitchen," Angela says as she smiles at Liz, who is speechless, shaking her head, holding the steering wheel tight. Liz speaks. "I can't believe this. I've never seen windows like that. And, my father was in construction. We lived in many old houses while he remodeled them or built new ones. This was constructed as a subdivision, with all the houses similar. I don't doubt anything you say anymore."

They are about to run out of daylight, but are too excited to stop. Continuing down the street again counting each home number, they come to discover that 410 Curry Avenue is now the site of a gas station. A complete validation cannot be made according to Angela, and no check marks go down next to her potato dream. But, she has no doubts her cellar and potatoes came from Curry Avenue. Pure adrenaline flows between Angela and Liz that day as they are led from one incredible validation to another. This Palm Sunday will always be a day to remember rebirth and resurrections.

Settlement

M onday, their last day in Lexington, finally arrives. The schedule is simple for that morning. They would spend a few hours at the County Clerk's office finding whatever is available and then follow up at the cemetery before finally heading back home around midday.

The County Clerk's office has very few people in it other than employees and law clerks when Angela and Liz arrive at their front door at 8:30. They wander down the halls, passing numerous county administration offices until finally reaching the land records office.

Inside, they find large shelves full of leather bound books labeled with numbers. Hoping the large books contain information for them, Angela and Liz begin to look around. Liz opts for the computer system, thinking it might help them more quickly find what they need.

Angela on the other hand is inexplicably drawn to a metal cabinet at the far left of the room. When she arrives to look at the large green leather bound books, the first thing she notices is their age. They look very old. The binders themselves quickly confirm her suspicions. They are labeled with dates from a century or more and the title "Deed and Mortgages" is hand painted in white on the spines.

She glances through the books, dating back to the late 1800s, and locates the index for the years 1918 to 1922. She is sure Klair bought her the house shortly after their marriage in 1919. This book would cover land conveyances for the first three years of their marriage, which is quite significant considering they were married just under four years.

To her relief, the index is alphabetized for all of the years it contains. She places the heavy book on the slanted table nearby and lets her finger guide her to the Ws. Past the Wiemans, Weisenbachs and Weisbrotts, she finds Weitzel, A.K. Indexed next to his name is a deed from Frances E. Beauchamp.

"Liz, I found something. Come here!" whispers Angela as she scribbles down the book and page number provided by the index. Liz arrives, shocked that she has found something so quickly. They just arrived! "Can you look up this deed while I search for more?" Angela asks.

"Sure," Liz says, taking the note from Angela and looking at the enormous shelves of oversized books that have not been opened in many years. Liz quickly finds the book on the shelf and struggles under its weight as she carries it to a table nearby. It lands with a large thud as others in the room turn their heads. She turns to the correct page and finds the deed, just as the index had promised. Liz begins to read, assessing its value with regard to any information she may already know from Angela's dreams.

Angela is searching in another index book for any indication of when Klair might have sold property when the silence of the room is shattered by a loud gasp from Liz. Liz grabs her mouth with both hands and slowly backs away from the larger-than-life book. Angela quickly leaves what she is doing to check on Liz. Liz can only point.

Angela looks down at the page, typed on a manual typewriter with fading ink, and begins to read the deed. On October 15, 1919, Frances Beauchamp, a widow, sold her house to Klair Weitzel. She had lived in it for fourteen years.

The house was not cheap, certainly not a house one would expect from a grocery store salesman. It cost $4,000.00, payable in two installments of $2,000 each. He paid the total balance only a year and a half later. It was a two-story brick house. And, it was specifically described as being located on the south side of East Maxwell Street.

It takes a moment for the ink on the page to sink into Angela and Liz's skin. It was another validation to add to a now heavy folder full of evidence to support Angela's dreams. Their trip became an instant success and neither could fathom how they managed to come upon so much information in so little time.

And now, in their first ten minutes at the County Clerk's office, they have found their coveted prize. With the entire morning still ahead, Liz decides to venture over to the other side of the office and start looking up wills, something that was on the to-do list, but of least importance to either of them. Angela begins searching records in the computer, and later looks through plot indexes of different subdivisions at the turn of the century.

Liz finds Klair's will, probated and registered in the books with other wills from the same year of his death, 1936. Klair left custody of their two children, Margaret Elizabeth and Charles, to Francine's sister, Margaret. At the time of his death, he is living next door to Francine's mother, who was still alive and living at 315 West Maxwell Street. Francine's mother had taken care of Klair and probated his will. Klair's own mother had passed away when he was only eight years old. Francine's mother took her place decades later, after his children lost their own mother, his wife. Life dealt him a terrible blow, but he found refuge in Francine's family and their many maternal figures.

Their work at the County Clerk's office a huge success, Angela and Liz gather up their new collection of evidence and head to the cemetery for one last goodbye. The day is bright and cheery, full of birds chirping and people going about their Monday morning business. As they drive away from the County Clerk's office, Angela feels caught in a strange matrix, sure that only she is seeing what she's seeing. She appreciates the simplicity of watching an older lady go to her mailbox. She finds joy in the simple act of watching the little details of life as Liz drives down Main Street. Is the older lady happy she can still walk to her mailbox? Is the college kid thankful he has a dog and that it didn't soil the carpet in his rented room? "We should all slow down to enjoy the simpler things in life. It ends too quickly," she thinks, filled with a new emotion she can't quite label.

The gates to the cemetery are open as Liz drives through them once again. She parks in the same spot as before and sits in the car waiting for Angela to say her goodbyes. She is starting to get comfortable sitting in libraries, reading about dead people and then visiting them in cemeteries. Even though they are dead, she feels as if she knows them. Just from knowing Angela, witnessing her experiencing their lives, she has been brought reluctantly into their loving fold. Liz is happy for Angela and notices a new sparkle in her friend's eye. She somehow knows her friend will be different from now on. She is healing, and for that Liz is deeply grateful.

Angela approaches the graves with two palms from St. Paul's Mass clutched in her hands. The reeds feel dry and smooth but filled with life despite their brown appearance. She stands before the grave of Francine's sister Margaret and thanks her for raising the children. She must have been a very special person. She goes next to the grave of Charles, Francine's son. She begins to speak softly as she places a palm at his grave. "Hi there. I brought you a palm from St. Paul's. I hope you loved that church as much as your mother did. I'm sorry you and Greta had to grow up without her. I can't imagine how lonely the two of you must have been. And, I hope you had a wonderful life." Her words are sincere with a tinge of regret. Angela has no recollection of Charles. Francine died when he was just a baby, nine months old.

She passes by Francine's grave and stands in front of Klair's. Kneeling down in front it, Angela closes her eyes and whispers, "Klair, I'm so sorry for all you had to go through. I never meant to hurt you. You were a wonderful husband, and I can tell you firsthand that Francine loved you with every part of her deepest soul. You were her everything. You mourned for her. Now I mourn for you." She closes her eyes as a teardrop spirals from her eyes onto the blades of grass next to his grave's marker.

"I brought you this palm. Yesterday was Palm Sunday and I went to St. Paul's for Mass. I noticed nobody puts anything on the graves here anymore because all the survivors are dead. So, since I'm alive and I can . . . I thought your grave deserved something special. I'll be back again to see you one day . . . In the meantime, I guess I'll just be seeing you in my dreams." She placed the dried palm in front of his grave, tucked between blades of grass at the base of his granite headstone.

With all the objectives of the trip completed, Angela and Liz take the road leading out of Lexington. Before they are entirely out of the city, Angela makes one last demand of her friend. "I want to stop at a nursery if you don't mind," she says to Liz.

"Sure. But why?"

"I just want to take something back with me from Kentucky. Something that will last."

At the nursery, Angela purchases the only pink rose bush they have left. She is not surprised there is only one, and feels nothing but absolute joy as she loads it back into the car. She doesn't tell Liz about her dream of Klair and the rose bush. It is private, and she wants to keep it that way. It would be her and Klair's memory to keep.

She decides it will be planted in her back yard, in memory of all the people she shared the weekend with who are no longer physically with her. Like all living things, the rose bush would appear dead during the winter, only to come back with beautiful roses during the spring and summer, a symbol of the circle of life, with blooms of love hanging from its familial branches.

The road back to Atlanta seems much shorter than the road to Lexington. Liz is eager to return home and looking forward to sleeping in her own bed. She is full of thoughts and knows her friend is no different. Angela drives this time, and Liz, bored with her novel, pulls out her notebook. "I want to see how many validations we received. You were right about everything. 100%."

"Not exactly. I interpreted that church dream as a wedding dream, when obviously it wasn't. She wore blue, not white."

"So? That was your interpretation that was wrong, not the dream itself. Everything about the dream checked out. And, she probably was wearing white. It was probably her confirmation rather than her wedding."

"Do they wear white then?" asks Angela.

"Yes, they do. And, someone who's not Catholic could easily think a kid is going to a wedding instead . . . It would also explain why you felt so Catholic at that moment staring up at the stained glass window."

"Okay. I'll take that. But, we still have to strike out the wedding part on my list."

"You can do that. I'm going to make a separate list and count."

Liz begins to write, sorting each validation according to the time it took place.

Internet Research

1. Name: Francine Donovan
2. Name: Klair
3. They were married.
4. During the turn of the century
5. Oldest child daughter
6. Railroad connection w/ her family

Liz's Business Trip

1. She was Catholic
2. He went by Klair v. Augustine

Final Trip: Day one

1. Church foyer matched (even though renovated)
2. Wood molding in church

3. Tall narrow stained glass windows
4. Front doors of church matched description

Day 2

1. Klair "prosperous business man"
2. Traveled after the wedding/honeymoon
3. Klair's family prominent (very)
4. Francine's family not prominent
5. Found socialite/rich Aunt
6. Hotel connection to Klair's family

Day 3

1. Stained glass window in St. Paul's foyer existed (fleur de lis/spades)
2. Park near house
3. Park fit description
4. 207 Woodland Avenue not her house
5. Proved she did not live at 315 W. Maxwell Street
6. Proved Woodland Avenue block was commercial
7. Fire station was on same corner

Day 4

1. Lived on E. Maxwell Street
2. On the south side
3. Park would have been to her right from a front bedroom window
4. House was two story
5. House was big/expensive ($4,000)
6. They had money (paid off in 1½ years)
7. Someone lived in the house previously (Ms. Beauchamp: 14 years).

"What about Curry Avenue? Can I count that since you found your small windows?" asks Liz. "No, I didn't find the house. That's just not close enough." Angela resists.

"And why don't you seem to care how she died?" Liz asks. Angela hesitates a moment and then speaks from her heart. "To be honest with you, I don't know. And, I don't care. You see, it's not her death that was important; it was her life and those she loved. We shouldn't be defined by how and when we die, or what job we put down on a census report. We are all so much more than that. We are the love we give others." Liz quietly considers Angela's words. She is impressed with her friend's progress throughout the journey. Liz knows that faced with the same situation, she would've done everything possible to find out how Francine died. She admires Angela's unique point of view.

Neither is quite sure what to make of it all. They only know that the dreams were in fact real. The rest, they would each have to figure out on their own, each carrying their own religious luggage and labels.

"So now that it's all true, I guess things will somehow be different," suggests Liz.

"How so?"

"Well, now that you have proved reincarnation to yourself, I guess you'll run off and be Hindu or Buddhist."

"I'm still afraid of those religion boxes."

"That's fair," says Liz, amazed Angela still holds resentment for her childhood religion.

"What about you, Ms. Catholic girl? What are you going to do?"

"I don't know if I would call it 'reincarnation' according to the typical definition. But, I believe in the dreams you had and I believe in you. I think God has worked some major miracles here. And, I think you are extremely psychic and had better start accepting it."

"What? You are kidding me." chuckles Angela.

"No. I'm not. You have a gift. Whether or not you were really Francine, you were able to pick up on everything about her life and how she felt. Something about this family has attached to you. And, you were psychic enough and stubborn enough to do all this work in return. Either way, it's a beautiful thing. You've learned so much from being Francine."

It was true. Angela had learned a great deal from seeing and feeling the world through Francine's eyes and emotions. Francine was more insecure than Angela, unsure of her place in society. She was ahead of her time, a professional working woman at the turn of the century, a spinster turned wife. She did not accept the transition easily, and Angela felt compassion for her struggles. She could understand her own grandparents' reluctance to accept the changes and fast pace of modern society. She was beginning to loathe it herself.

The park they had visited was so peaceful and quiet. There were no radio or car sounds, only nature and the pure, beautiful sounds of happy children. From now on, Angela will reserve moments in her day for silence. She will ride home without the radio on. She will turn everything off in her house and sit in silence, accepting it as the gift it really is. She has learned a lot. Liz is right.

"So what about your other friends and family? What are they going to say?" asks Liz.

"Probably a lot, but I hope they understand this is not something satanic or demonic. It's about love. You don't have to believe in the supernatural to believe in love."

"That's not what their churches will say." reminds Liz.

"No. They'll say its Satan sending me these messages of life and love from the depths of hell. Funny thing is, it's all semantics. They preach 'God spoke to me . . . God whispered in my ear', but I ask, how is that any different from what happens to a psychic? It's the same! And they say, 'God has appointed unto us Angels for our protection . . . guardian angels'. New Age people call your guardian angel a spirit guide. It's the same thing! And there are tons of instances in the bible related to dream interpretations. Why would it be okay in the bible and not okay now? If God spoke to biblical people through their dreams, why can't He speak to us now in our dreams? I just don't get it.

"And, the very document they hold as the sacred text, they readily admit was 'inspired' by God through the hands of man. Hello! That's automatic writing! We are all speaking the same language; we're just bogged down in vocabulary. One word will send you to hell, the other to heaven. We all have been given the power to experience grace. We just have to start paying attention. It's that simple."

"So, will life be different now that you choose to believe in reincarnation?" Liz asks simply.

"Yes," replies Angela thoughtfully. "I think so . . . more peaceful. And, I didn't choose to believe in reincarnation, it chose me."

Epilogue

There were no celebrations when Liz and Angela returned home. No high school bands cheered for them or paraded next to their car as it arrived into town. They drove safely by Christian and Baptist churches. They waved at children in the back seats of mothers' cars. The mothers smiled back at them, thinking they were normal people. Angela preferred it that way. So did Liz. Angela shared the secrets of Lexington with very few people. She felt it was her own experience and its application to her spiritual beliefs was of no concern to anyone else.

Brent was speechless for the first time in his life as Angela went through the pieces of evidence she meticulously catalogued the weeks after her return from Lexington. He was excited for her and thankful his wife could now rest. Angela's mother and father were equally speechless. Luther, her father, summed it up at dinner one night over a bowl of salsa and chips at their favorite Mexican restaurant.

"I've heard of these things happening to people before, but never to anybody I trusted." Those words encompassed the feelings of the few people Angela allowed to know, including Liz.

But she still wondered "Why me?" She felt a security and privilege in anonymity, as though she had received a precious gift, proof of some form of afterlife and confirmation of the eternal nature of love. She now understood the beauty and purity of complete normalcy.

Angela's rose bush had bloomed all summer long, with full pink aromatic roses hanging off its branches. If the breeze was in the right direction, she could sometimes smell them as she sat on her back porch. But soon, the summer would begin its yearly retreat and everyone would prepare for the beginning of fall, clearing away dead leaves fallen from trees that months later will spring forth new life.

The harvest moon, full and brighter than it has been in decades dances through her backyard in October of 2003, six months since her trip to Lexington, as Angela lies motionless in her bed, eyes wide open. "Why me?" she thinks to herself again. "Out of all the people in the world why me?" She raises her arm to look at the time on her watch as her husband sleeps soundly by her side. It is 3:00 in the morning.

Their room is illuminated by the full moon and Angela can see every detail. She rises from bed, grabs her robe, steps over the dog and starts down the stairs to the kitchen. Taking a piece of paper off the refrigerator door, she grabs a pen from the counter, a match book from the drawer, and goes outside. She has an idea.

The rose bush sits quietly in the corner of her back yard, feeling more at home now. Its branches are relaxed, its Kentucky potted soil long mixed with the Georgia red clay. The night air is refreshing and unseasonably warm for October. The leaves that have fallen crunch beneath Angela's feet as she walks barefooted on the cool earth. She kneels down in front of the rose bush, her knees touching the earth for the first time since Klair's grave. She feels completely grounded, ready to move onto the next phase of her life, wherever it may take her.

She takes out a pen and pad and begins to write. Tears flow freely down her cheeks as she allows her soul to bleed. Her hand moves quickly as words are released from deep within. Several minutes pass as she writes without stopping. Finally, she sighs a breath of relief, folds the paper and places it in a ceramic bowl lying abandoned next to the rose bush. Angela then takes a match, strikes it on the box, and lights the paper on fire.

With two outstretched hands, she lifts the ceramic bowl towards the heavens, instinctively bowing her head with respect. "Thank you for allowing me to feel your love. Please take my words."

Angela remains silent, allowing the universe to absorb the words which now float towards heaven imbedded in smoke. For she knows nothing in her life could warrant the experience they allowed her to have. She would never deserve their gift or be able to repay them properly. She hoped her words would be enough.

My Dearest:

I can see you fade before me
with the morning light.
I feel your embrace lighten
as I slip back into consciousness.

I have fallen
in love and out of time with you.
I awake to your smell,

still lingering after a successful night
  of desperate searching.

My feelings for you make me realize that our
  souls are endless,
our capacity for love boundless.
With every dream of you, I feel touched by
  the heavens,
blessed yet again by your presence.

A new understanding purifies my soul,
calming my waters and illuminating my core.
Thank you.
By the grace of heaven my turbulent waters
  have turned to glass.

God has restored my soul.

SOMETIMES DREAMS DON'T COME TRUE . . .

BECAUSE THEY ALREADY ARE . . .

If you would like to order additional copies of
CHOSEN TO BELIEVE

You may write to us for more information and possible discounts:

1. Simply clip out or photocopy the form below with your name and address filled in and mail the form to the address below. Or, call our toll free number 1-800-583-1439

> The Pink Elephant Press
> P.O. Box 1153
> Jonesboro, GA 30237-1153

2. Or, fax the form below to our toll free fax number: 1-800-583-1439

3. Or, visit us online at: www.thepinkelephantpress.com to place your order on our secure server.

I AM INTERESTED IN PURCHASING
ADDITIONAL COPIES OF
CHOSEN TO BELIEVE

Full Name _____
          (First)   (Last)

Company Name _____
  (if applicable)

Street Address _____

City, State, Zip _____

I am interested in purchasing at bulk discount: _____ yes _____ no

---

Bulk purchase discounts are available. Special books, booklets or book excerpts can also be created to fit your specific needs. For information contact Marketing Department, The Pink Elephant Press, P.O. Box 1153, Jonesboro, GA 20237-1153 (800) 583-1439

Printed in the United States
37278LVS00006B/13-144